Putin's Bo

This book is about truth and lies. For the truth about KGB agent Vladimir Putin's world, explore the lies of his stamp men.

A doctor and his nephew co-founded the Gulag. A loving father was a kidnapper, a mathematician was a murderer. A cafeteria manager tortured teachers, a lawyer ran a slave-labor camp, and a circus performer burned villages. Men's faces on simple postage stamps reveal the history and consequences of the Soviet police state and show how that history moves into our present with two decades of Putin's governance.

The stamp men were celebrated as counterintelligence heroes, but they were killers. They were Chekists, secret policemen who flooded a nation with fear, who enabled the Soviet Union but then destroyed it.

If Russia is to be admired, peaceful and vibrant, its government must correspond honestly with its people and the world. Instead, more than 160 stamps since 1992 have direct or indirect Cheka connections. The stamp men are bright red warning lights telling us of dangerous weaknesses—suspicion and self-deception. This book calculates in blunt terms the staggering price that has been paid.

Mark Pruett (Ph.D., University of Illinois; M.B.A. and B.S., University of North Carolina) is an experienced university teacher and scholar in strategic management, international business, creativity, entrepreneurship and innovation. His academic publications cover subjects like leadership character, education, competitive strategy, and technological change. He began as an international consultant writing research studies for dozens of overseas companies, and he has a life-long love of travel and history. One of his ancestors was the famous adventurer Moritz Benyovszky. American's national anthem, *The Star Spangled Banner*, was first performed in 1814 in Baltimore at a theatrical play about Benyovszky, who escaped a Siberian prison in 1771 by stealing a Russian government ship.

Info: www.markwpruett.com

Patrol boat "Chekist" on the Moscow-Volga Canal.
Tens of thousands of forced laborers died digging the canal.
(Photo: Alexander Egorov, army chief of staff, shot in 1939) [235]

Patrol boat "Chekist II" at Solovki camp,
birthplace of the Gulag forced-labor system. [236]

Putin's Boys
The Stamp Men

MARK PRUETT

ARTICLE58
IMPRINTS

Putin's Boys: The Stamp Men

Copyright Mark Pruett, 2020. All rights reserved.

Published by Article58 Imprints, Tryon, North Carolina

Cover credits

"What is the cost of lies?" Opening and closing line from the Home Box Office (HBO) television drama series <u>Chernobyl</u>, 2019.

"Let there be floods of blood." From "Blood for Blood", <u>Red Gazette</u>, 1 September 1918.

Russian 2002 stamps RFK675, 677, 679, 681, 683, and 684

Luhansk (Lugansk) December 2018 stamps

Cover artwork & design copyright Mark Pruett

Typefaces

Cover: Jakob
Text: Baskerville Old Face

ISBN 978-1-7344989-0-5 paperback

*Dedicated to those destroyed
by the world's stamp men,
and to children deformed by the world
into stamp men.*

Contents

Photos and Illustrations

You, the living, you step on the bones of the dead.

Janis Zile, Gulag camp survivor *[189]*

To the Reader

This book is about truth—and lies. To seek truth about Vladimir Putin's world, explore the lies of his stamp men.

A set of seemingly simple Russian postage stamps reveals the history and consequences of the Soviet police state, and demonstrates how that history moves into our present with the government of president Vladimir Putin, career counter-intelligence agent for the KGB.

The project grew from the very tiniest of seeds—two mere sentences, hidden in the preface to Prof. Donald Rayfield's engrossing Stalin and His Hangmen, which mention a set of Russian stamps from 2002. [226]   I bought the stamps and studied them in my spare time, not realizing how far this would lead me into the lives and meaning of these men.

I thank the memory of my father, a Depression-era boy from a small mountain town who rose to lead the world's greatest music library. He loved the printed word and history, and taught me to treasure human beings and rarely-opened, long-forgotten volumes. So, too, I thank my mother, a stateless war refugee who quite literally made her own passport. She has spent her life teaching, studying, and playing music, and has taught me the adventure of maps, the importance of knowing ancestors, and the joy of research which charts its own course. In addition, my parents taught their children to love travel and the unknown. My faults are my own, but the good in me and my boundless curiosity are the gifts of wonderful parents.

The stamp men

Dedicated to the 80th anniversary of the counterintelligence unit of the security organs

Outstanding counterintelligence officers

One must sometimes correct history.

Joseph Stalin [155]

Gulag co-founder   *Kidnapper*   *Rebellion crusher*

Mass exiler   *Inquisitor*   *The human plague*

Enforcer   *Gulag co-founder*   *Enforcer*

Enforcer   *Torturer*   *Enforcer*

1. They were killers

Иди и смотри (Idi i smotri) — Come and see.
Book of Revelation 6:1 [178]

And ye shall know the truth and the truth shall make you free.
John VIII - XXXII [180]

THEY WERE KILLERS, these men on postage stamps. They killed men, women, children. They arrested, tortured, and exiled them. They beat, shot, gassed, starved, and froze them. They worked them to death. They threw them out windows. They spilled torrents of blood and in the end they were killed, too.

Less than two years after former KGB officer Vladimir Putin's first election as president, the Russian post office issued in 2002 a sheet of stamps to commemorate Soviet-era counterintelligence agents.

The sheet does not name the stamp men's employer. There is no need. Any present-day Russian, or any person from any part of the former Soviet Union, is a person whose very *existence* has been shaped by these and other stamp men. Their parents, grandparents, and great-grandparents were intimately acquainted with such men, whether as onlookers, victims, or participants—or in all three roles.

Can we say it is a waste of time to study faces on stamps?

We cannot. Business executives, intelligence analysts, news correspondents and officials must learn about people and places, and assess what it would be like to work with, for, or against them.

1

The 2002 stamps were issued one week before the 80th anniversary of a 6 May 1922 meeting to create a new internal unit in the secret police to house long-running efforts against "the subversive activities of foreign intelligence services, foreign émigré centers, smuggling, illegal border crossing and political banditry". [22]

Can the stamp men explain a century of politics, economics, and foreign relations? Indeed, stamps send messages to a nation and the world. They deliver more than letters: they convey perceptions, aspirations, and the atmosphere in which official decisions are made.

The stamp men's employer is Vladimir Putin's long-time employer, the state security apparatus, now known as the FSB and SVR, previously known in Soviet times by a bewildering, ever-changing series of acronyms: KGB, MVD, MGB, NKGB, NKVD, OGPU, GPU and, before that, the VCheka or Cheka, the All-Russia Extraordinary Commission for Combating Counter-Revolution [etc.], founded in 1917 during the Russian Revolution and Civil War.

The Cheka's founder and leader was "Iron" Felix Dzerzhinsky, working to fulfill the mandate given him by Vladimir Lenin. Employees were Chekists, their emblem an unsheathed sword and shield. Official structures and names change, but the song remains the same. The emblem and nickname survive. State security agencies are intuitively understood as the Cheka, and state security employees are still Chekists. Dzerzhinsky was a Chekist. Putin is a Chekist.

Does a passing thunderstorm matter once a surging current has carried its load of organic debris under a bridge?

Should we seek what was washed away, find the high water mark, inspect the bridge's footings, and watch the stream and sky for evidence of the storm's return?

How do we deal with complicated, painful memories?

For people unfamiliar with the stamp men or their agency, the stamps mean nothing. For some, the stamps convey an admirable but hazy past. For others, the stamps are reminders of a complex history revealed by diving into bloody depths.

We—individuals, groups, societies—want and need happiness, confidence, stability, and a sense of a positive future. How should we find and develop such things when the past is awash with blood? Some argue that remembrance can help heal deep wounds, others that laying things to rest is better. Regardless, we need honesty and knowledge—a better understanding of historical fact—before we can make wise and healthy choices about remembrance and forgetfulness.

So, let us glide down history's currents and find the 2002 stamp men. Later, we will find a new set of stamp men commemorated at the very end of 2018. At the end of our journey, we will arrive at the utterly bleak central irony of the stamp men.

The stamp men are part of a pattern. As the Appendix of this book shows, post-Soviet Russia has issued more than 160 stamps that have connections, direct or indirect, to the Cheka.

The 2002 and 2018 stamp men are not about an increasingly distant and irrelevant past. Although they are tied most directly to two specific periods of Soviet and Russian history—1918 to 1938 and World War II (the Great Patriotic War)—they illuminate a fearful and fearsome century which leads inexorably into our present.

By suggesting that the stamp men are heroes, the history of the 20th century is being deliberately and profoundly distorted by the government of Vladimir Putin.

The stamp men were not heroes. They were killers.

Come and see.

3

Before we begin our journey, a couple of comments are in order to help set the journey's context.

First, the stamp men's stories reflect diverse materials. Some draw more on relatives and locations, others official records and acts. We are studying people from a long-lived, often violent organization which has generally sought to conceal or destroy revealing material. Documenting details of each stamp man's story is important for developing a truthful account, yet it also is important not to get lost in the details and miss the broader lessons from the combination of the stamp men's stories.

Second, one term deserves particular mention for its distinct meaning, which not be familiar to all readers. "Repression", the act of being repressed, means the punishment of individuals, groups, and entire segments of society for political reasons. It is different than consequences for what would be considered normal, "ordinary" crimes, *e.g.*, bar fights or embezzlement. Repression, however, is a consequence of anything, including an ordinary crime, deemed a political crime hostile to the state and thus punishable. If the reader wishes, a quick Internet search for "Article 58" of the Soviet criminal code makes clear that *anything* could be deemed a political crime— including family relationships, personal thoughts or just being unaware of something. Being repressed might mean an arrest for something, a court event, and sentencing, but many people were repressed without such time-consuming formalities. The word's meaning is fraught with suffering and death.

2. The cost of lies

No great culture can be based on a crooked relationship to the truth.

Robert Musil, 1935 *[69]*

TO KNOW THE COST of lies, we must recognize that postage stamps both depend on and influence a sense of self and a sense of dignity. This seems healthy...unless the stamps are based on a crime.

Sense of self

At first glance, the 2002 stamp men are a nice gesture toward Vladimir Putin to honor the place where the new president built his career. Had Putin been a cosmonaut instead of a spy, we might have seen new stamps at that time for Laika the dog, Yuri Gagarin and Valentina Tereshkova. After university, Putin started working in KGB counterintelligence. He worked for the KGB for sixteen years. In the late 1990s, he briefly ran its successor, the FSB.

A second look is more telling. The stamp men show that the Soviet Union may be gone, but the Cheka's sword and shield continue to protect Russia. In the Soviet Union, police and intelligence agents were part of popular mythology. Putin and the rest of the Union grew up with such stories in books and movies. A rough parallel in America is FBI agent Eliot Ness's work to bring the gangster Al Capone to justice.

Stories like these create positive images and may help focus public perception on important issues, whether foreign interference or

5

organized crime. After all, any organization—a family, a business, a government—seeks pride and purpose in its past. Families want to hear about ancestors, business employees want to admire corporate achievements. American police look up to role models like Eliot Ness, and it is natural that Russian counterintelligence agents, who lived through the traumatic collapse of the Soviet Union, want to feel proud of their spy-catching predecessors.

The third examination is the most important. We find lessons in the faces of six young men—mostly boys, really—who joined a new organization promising a radiant future. Their work was bloody but felt important. They went on distant journeys and to the nexus of power. The stamp men did not represent Soviet power, they <u>were</u> Soviet power. Heady stuff, indeed, for impressionable young minds.

In truth, though, the stamp men built, worked in and finally were destroyed by an agency which served as a control mechanism but was itself difficult to control, in a larger institutional system fueled by suspicion and self-deception. The commemoration of the stamp men and their agency represents an authorized, politicized, romanticized, and sanitized hagiography which is, fundamentally, a lie.

This false history matters. Families, companies, governments—all are organizations. When we belong to an organization, or study one, or have dealings with one, history is useful. For a fuller view, we also must grasp the organization's beliefs and desires regarding its history. Facts, beliefs and desires will not align neatly, and this will explain major sources of conflict, poor decision-making, and adverse results.

For example, Vladimir Putin and others claim that his grandfather Spiridon Ivanovich cooked for three important figures—Vladimir Lenin, his widow Nadezhda Krupskaya, and Joseph Stalin. True or not, Putin's claim is a bid to be stamped with historical legitimacy, a desire to be imbued with a positive glow from decidedly mythical and dishonest images of Lenin and Stalin. For anyone with a conspiratorial view of Soviet history, Putin's culinary claim also may be a warning—some scholars believe Stalin poisoned Lenin's widow through food and may have killed her husband as well.

Today's workers in Russia's intelligence agencies, capable humans imbued with feelings of purpose and tradition, look out the same office windows as did the men on the postage stamps. Surely, though, the windowframes still help define the view and, as we shall see, the ponderous headquarters building still casts its shadow.

No view of history, not even this tale of the stamp men, is entirely accurate. However, no matter who and where we are, we are the offspring of diverse and particular histories, shaped by the consequences of the past. We cannot understand much about *why* we are who we are, or make truly wise and informed decisions, unless we know something about the truth of the past, unless we have a truer sense of self. Historical facts, our beliefs, our desires—they all matter.

Sense of dignity

The 2002 stamps were created by Boris Semenovich Ilyukhin (b. 23 January 1947), founder of the Moscow "Old School" art academy art school and chief stamp designer in post-Soviet Russia. As of late 2019 the stamp men do not appear in Ilyykhin's extensive personal online gallery of his decades of stamp work. Still, in a BBC interview (which misstates his name as Mitukin), Ilyukhin said: "We're starting to realise in Russia that not everything in our history was bad. These were honest, decent citizens. Some of them were even geniuses. They helped protect our country and our people." *[18, 67, 68]*

Ilyukhin thus tacitly admits that much of Soviet history was awful. His comments also demonstrate that Russia believes good things about its past, even when some of those beliefs are not true. Seventy-five years of Soviet news, literature, school, art, music, movies, monuments, names of buildings, streets, and cities, and postage stamps—all controlled by a centralized state—embedded remarkably distorted perceptions of the past deep into society's memory.

The stamps highlight an understandable motive—the need to see or find positive elements in past events. Enduring suffering for no good reason can crush hope. Causing suffering for no positive purpose should feel profoundly shameful.

Certainly, lies may seem desirable, beneficial, even necessary for our own well-being and dignity. Perhaps, for the sake of the past, present, and future, it is better to find more desirable justifications, even false ones, for what we endure and, especially, for what we cause. Without pursuing truth, though, we cannot even freely decide which lies we will tell to ourselves, and a healthy sense of dignity will remain elusive. To pursue that truth, we must reveal a crime.

<u>Lenin's crime</u>

Ilyukhin's 2002 stamp men were not "honest, decent citizens" protecting the country and its people. To secure their political party's power, they used torture, prison, and murder to frighten people into permanent submission. Fear was the core operational principle of the agency which in a later form was Vladimir Putin's employer.

In the decades before World War I, Russia was rapidly changing from a semi-feudal agrarian society to an industrializing one. Railroad systems and telecommunications networks were growing fast. Foreign investment was substantial, heavy industry was booming, and new technology and ideas were pouring in. Oil and other exports were making the country rich. If Russia could evolve and make suitable internal adaptations, it could look forward to a bright and prosperous twentieth century.

However, Russia's governance structure was not keeping up with the changes. Despite reform efforts, the vast country's festering economic and political inequalities and injustices were not being addressed well by Russia's rigid bureaucracy, stratified society, and the remarkably inept Tsar Nicholas II. The slide into bloody World War I made clear that this tsar was incapable of leading Russia toward better government. 1917 brought rebellion and full-fledged civil war.

In this war over Russia's future, Vladimir Lenin and his Bolshevik party wanted a Marxist communist society, with themselves at the helm. Lenin created the Cheka in December 1917 to help the Bolsheviks win the civil war, and put Felix Dzerzhinsky in charge. Deliberately and completely freed from legal restraints or prior norms, the Cheka embarked on a campaign to overwhelm any opposition with simple, unrelenting, unthinkable violence—the Red Terror. One year later, on 19 December 1918, the Cheka placed its counterintelligence efforts in a new unit, the Special Department, to gather intelligence and eliminate opponents. Twenty years later the Cheka would cement Stalin's rule with the Great Terror purge.

For decades, acting on ignorance, fear, and opportunism, Chekists and their successors destroyed tens of millions of human beings. What they touched, they made worse—agriculture, industry, science, art, literature, foreign relations, national defense, community, family, love. By killing farmers, they expanded famines. By killing teachers and scientists, managers and engineers, poets and musicians, they lobotomized a nation and devastated its economy and culture. By killing the Soviet Union's own diplomats, intelligence agents, military officers and soldiers before, during, and after World War II, they weakened the country, increased suffering, and made a mess of international relations. By pitting neighbor against neighbor, they destroyed human ties and the basic fabric of society.

By killing those who disagreed, were suspected of disagreeing, or might disagree, and by killing or otherwise punishing people associated with actual, possible, suspected, or imagined dissidents, Chekists made their agency, their government, their citizens—their entire society—ever more inflexible and unresponsive.

Like people everywhere, many Soviet citizens were good people, honest and dedicated, but their goodness was subordinated to a system which fomented fear and eroded human society. It was "impossible for anybody to trust anybody else." *[172]*

The result was almost incomprehensible. For decades people would lie to each other and to themselves—at home, in school, at work, in government. The country was denied the benefits of information, discussion and debate. Whatever was not officially supported at any given moment was discouraged and denied.

Reality has, however, a way of making itself known in time. The problems eventually became too great to be buried or papered-over by a culture of denial. Almost three-quarters of a century after its birth, the Soviet Union, one of the world's two "super-powers", could not resolve a host of profoundly obvious problems—social, political, bureaucratic, military, technological, economic, environmental.

It could not address these problems before they became overwhelming because it was afraid to adequately acknowledge them. Despite desperate measures which, as such measures often do, came too late, the government of the world's largest country just collapsed, in large part because it simply could not stop *lying*.

Lenin's desperate, arrogant, sociopathic act—creating the Cheka to terrify a nation into submission—may be the single most catastrophic thing ever done by the Soviet Union. His willingness to kill debate, to murder truth, was *the* defining Soviet crime.

The cost

What, then, is the cost of lies?

Valery Legasov, a leading Soviet scientist who helped resolve and study the Soviet Union's disastrous 1986 nuclear reactor explosion in Chernobyl, was the deputy director of the Kurchatov Institute, established in 1943 by secret police chief Lavrenty Beria to develop nuclear weapons. The Chernobyl disaster was itself the direct result of a Chekist society—flaws in design, operation, and response were made worse by secrecy and institutionalized fear.

Two years after the explosion, Legasov killed himself. He found new life in 2019 as a lead character in the HBO television documentary-drama series Chernobyl. His speech in the climactic courtroom scene is scalpel-sharp:

"[O]ur secrets and our lies. They're practically what define us. When the truth offends, we lie and lie until we can no longer remember it is even there. But it is still there. Every lie we tell incurs a debt to the truth. Sooner or later, that debt is paid."

It does not matter that this speech was created for a television script. Each sentence helps us cut with exquisite precision to the heart of the matter of the stamp men:

The delayed and distorted development of the world's largest nation. The collapse of the Soviet socio-political-economic system and the emergence of a malformed post-Soviet offspring. The repression of human connections and society's ability to adapt to events and conditions. Tens of millions of deaths and ruined lives. The loss of dignity and self.

This is the cost of the stamp men. This is the cost of lies.

3. The map

Long live...the unsheathed sword of the working class!

J.V. Stalin, open letter to children, 1932

The stamp sheet border:

A, M   *The Lubyanka, secret police headquarters.*

B   *Operation Trust: early Soviet counterintelligence.*

C, L   *Dedications to the organization and agents.*

D, K   *Counterintelligence badges showing agency evolution.*

The stamp men:

E, F, G, H, I, J   *Early Soviet counterintelligence agents:*

Artuzov, Demidenko, Olsky, Puzitsky, Styrne, and Syroezhkin

4. The border

The Soviet nation is surrounded by a ring of invaders.

Pioneer Truth, 21 December 1932

WE MUST give credit to Boris Ilyukhin, the perceptive stamp designer. The border of the stamp sheet is filled with symbols of border defense and counterintelligence—the headquarters of the secret police, secret operation files, and dedications and badges to commemorate agency history.

<u>The Lubyanka</u>

Moscow's most famous address is the Kremlin, its most frightening the Lubyanka. Originally built as headquarters for an insurance company at the end of the 19th century, the new Soviet government in 1917 allocated it to the Cheka for offices and a prison. Thousands of people were pulled in for interrogation, while bureaucrats on other floors managed government purges, wholesale relocations of swaths of the country's citizenry, foreign espionage work and the intricate Gulag system of slave labor camps. The building grew into an enormous block-sized complex with internal courtyards and vehicle passageways. It has served secret police branches for more than a century. A makeover of the building's exterior began in the 1940s—it took more than forty years to finish and reach its present appearance.

Stamp border: The Lubyanka when the Cheka moved in

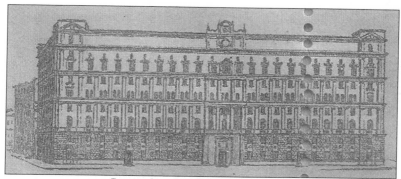

Stamp border: The Lubyanka today

Operation Trust

Trust: original 2nd Part file cover

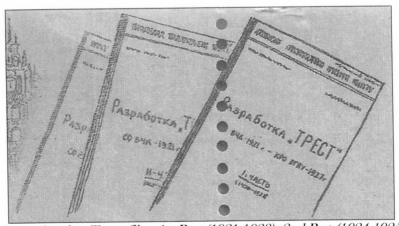

Stamp border: Trust, files, 1st Part (1921-1923), 2nd Part (1924-1925)

Counterintelligence operations *Trust* and *Syndicate-2* have been studied and mythologized for decades. The Cheka started Trust in 1921, and the OGPU finished it in 1927. Syndicate-2 ran more or less concurrently. The operations created false organizations and information to uncover enemies.

In *Trust*, British agent Sidney Reilly was lured and kidnapped. He was interrogated in Moscow by at least three stamp men—Artuzov, Styrne, and Syroezhkin, each of whom we will soon meet. A conveyor belt of rotating interrogators denied him sleep for days on end. He was rattled by at least one mock execution.

Internal reports to stamp man Styrne indicate that Reilly was shot on 5 November 1925. One agent wounded him with a shot in the back. Stamp man Syroezhkin killed him with a shot to the chest and he was buried in a Lubyanka courtyard. Perhaps he is still there. *[53]*

In *Syndicate-2*, anti-Bolshevik expatriate Boris Savinkov was lured back. During or after interrogation, he was thrown out an upper-floor Lubyanka window by stamp men Syroezhkin and Puzitsky, and possibly their boss Felix Dzerzhinsky. The non-voluntary nature of Savinkov's brief flight was known as early as 1926. *[166, p. 109]*

The newer, semi-official explanation of the event, in which the valiant stamp men tried to save Savinkov from self-defenestration, is absurd. Occam's Razor applies, with three reasonable alternatives in this case. One, they dangled him outside the window and lost their grip (unlikely). Two, they dangled then let him fall (likely). Three, they simply threw him out (equally likely).

In Soviet Gulag camp slang, someone reduced to impending death through starvation and overwork was a *dokhodyaga* (доходяга), most often translated as "goner". A more accurate translation is an arriver or reacher. Euphemistic prisoner slang often made for bitter humor— a dead prisoner was said to have "fully reached Communism". When

Boris Savinkov departed a Lubyanka window for his final destination, he needed only a couple of seconds to fully reach Communism on the inner courtyard pavement—a true *dokhodyaga*, indeed.

One unintended consequence of secretive yet expansive operations like Trust and Syndicate-2 was that Soviet agents abroad unwittingly sent disinformation back home. Coupled with the compartmentalization, fear, employee turnover, and administrative disorder which increasingly characterized Soviet bureaucracies throughout the 1930s, the result was a government remarkably ill-equipped to assess or act on intelligence data.

The proof was in the pudding. A few years later, in June of 1941, Soviet agents reported to Moscow truthfully and in detail where and when Germany would soon attack. They were disbelieved. Military commanders on the western border were afraid to act without authorization from Moscow and did little to re-position their forces and equipment. Germany simply destroyed most of the Soviet air force on the ground and within days had killed or captured hundreds of thousands of Red Army soldiers.

Eventually, the Soviet Union would repel the invaders, but only with the help of American industrial might and the military forces of the Allies. Without this help and the blood of tens of millions of Soviet soldiers and civilians, the Soviet government would have died.

Certainly, Soviet citizens did not deserve the terrible suffering inflicted on them by the Germans, and Adolf Hitler's awful socio-political experiment did not deserve to survive.

However, the stamp men's stories will show the suffering the Soviet government had already inflicted on its citizens, and would inflict on them in history's largest war. The Soviet government did not deserve to survive, either. But, it did, and the Cheka cemented its own role as the nexus of institutionalized fear.

Dedications and badges

80-летию контрразведывательных подразделений органов безопасности посвящается

Dedicated to the 80th anniversary of the counterintelligence unit of the security organs

Выдающиеся контрразведчики 1922-1937 гг.

Outstanding counterintelligence officers 1922-1937

1917's VCheka (ВЧК) became the GPU (ГПУ) in 1922. The sword-and-shield insignia was overlaid with the Soviet hammer and sickle. The fifth anniversary Roman-numeral V is also a Latin alphabet double-entendre for VCheka. It is filled with official Soviet blood-red enamel. Each of the 2002 stamp men received this badge.

1917-1922 VChK-GPU

As shown in the eighty year anniversary badge below, the **GPU** became the **OPGU**. Counterintelligence Operations (**KRO**) became the **KGB**'s Second Main Directorate (**VGU**), which turned into the **FSB**'s Directorate of Counter-intelligence Operations (**UKRO**), and then the more recent Department of Counterintelligence (**DKR**). [24]

The anniversary badge is based on a standard Federal Security Service (**FSB**) emblem, which is derived from the Russian Federation coat of arms, which itself comes from Imperial Russia's emblem of a royal double eagle and a horseback rider (St. George) slaying a serpent/dragon. The enamel is blue.

For some reason, whether accidental or deliberate, the horseback rider on the **KRO** badge and other **FSB** badges faces to the left. In contrast, on the Russian state coat-of-arms, the rider faces right.

Eighty years of counterintelligence units
KRO-VGU-UKRO-DKR

5. The stamp men

Человек человеку волк—Chelovek cheloveku volk.

Man is wolf to man.

IN THE CENTER of the 2002 stamp sheet are six young agents in the early history of Soviet counterintelligence—the stamp men:
Artur Artuzov, counterintelligence chief and Gulag co-founder
Nikolai Demidenko, kidnapper
Jan Olsky, rebellion crusher
Sergei Puzitsky, mass deporter and slave camp commander
Vladimir Styrne, inquisitor of starving peasants
Grigory Syroezhkin, the human plague

Artuzov, Puzitsky, and Syroezhkin have brief biographies on the website of present-day Russia's foreign intelligence service, the SVR, which in administrative shuffling is now separate from the federal security service, the FSB. Olsky is commemorated in the leaders section of the website of Belarus's secret police. As of 2020, Belarus still chooses to call its agency the KGB. [23, 2]

The 2002 stamp men emerged during the Russian Revolution and Civil War. Puzitsky may be the only one with significant "normal" military front-line service—after he graduated from military school, he commanded an artillery unit. Syroezhkin was in the Red Army but quickly moved to tribunal work, and Artuzov apparently ran a unit of conscripted soldiers for several months before moving to "liquidating" traitors. The others—Demidenko, Olsky, Styrne—joined military tribunals before moving to the Cheka's tribunals. Finding Soviet enemies may have been more interesting work, and it certainly offered more safety, comfort, food, and opportunity than being a regular front-line Red Army soldier.

The stamp men soon found an unending supply of spies and counter-revolutionaries. Certainly, some were genuine military opponents and spies. Most were ordinary people who did not want Soviet freem and were appalled by its violent imposition.

As youths, the stamp men came from different places and backgrounds, but together they formed a young cohort in a new organization, the Cheka. The lure was irresistible—they would be part of a secret and unfettered agency, the sword and shield, the armed political enforcer and defender of a new government struggling to impose its will on an enormous territory. Opportunity, excitement, even family ties drew them to the Cheka.

Each of the stamp men found a different door into the Cheka, the agency which would define them for two decades. Artuzov was a cheese-maker's son. He was multilingual, well-educated, and a noted planner and organizer. Demidenko was from Ukraine and boldly staged a daytime street kidnapping in France. Olsky was a Polish doctor's son who ended his career managing cafeterias. Puzitsky graduated law school and wrote a detailed report about weaknesses in Cheka operations. Styrne began his career as a census mathematician. Syroezhkin started as a circus performer in Georgia before traveling the Soviet Union and Europe for almost two decades.

As part of the initial Cheka cohort, the stamp men often worked together at the core of the GPU's new counter-intelligence department. Artuzov, the eldest, became chief. They were all quite young at the outset—Artuzov barely thirty, the rest in their twenties.

When the Cheka became the GPU, they each received the previously mentioned 5-year Cheka-GPU sword-and-shield service badge. The badge numbers reflected one's importance. The Cheka's founder Felix Dzerzhinsky received badge number 1. Artuzov was number 33, Syroezhkin 120, Demidenko 121, Puzitsky 122, Styrne 353, and Olsky 369. Artuzov's uncle Mikhail Kedrov was number 52, and Kedrov's foster son Johann Tubala was 354. [175]

Eventually, each of the 2002 stamp men found the same exit out of the Cheka. Demidenko died first, likely by murder. The other five were shot and cremated, their remains dumped with thousands more in a large ash pit for executed prisoners known as Donskoye cemetery's Common Grave Number 1, only several miles from the Cheka's headquarters.

Execution, cremation, and a common grave provided a distinctly Soviet and communal end for these early enforcers of Bolshevik communism. Before they were killed, the stamp men were killers. Their arms were, in the self-descriptive words of the Soviet Union's future leader Nikita Khrushchev, "up to the elbows in blood."

Artur Khristianovich Artuzov

18 February 1891 - 21 August 1937
Counterintelligence chief, co-founder of the Gulag

Artuzov's bland SVR biography says he earned a degree in metallurgy, joined in 1918 "a commission that established Soviet power in the north of Russia", then rose in the Cheka to manage counter-intelligence operations, including Trust and Syndicate-2. [23]

Artuzov was born Frauchi but changed his name to sound more Russian. He was born in the Kashin district a hundred-odd miles north of Moscow. His parents were from Switzerland, and his father a cheese-maker. In 1917, Artuzov was recruited by his uncle Mikhail Sergeyevich Kedrov, who was married to a sister of Artuzov's mother. As commissar for the Demobilization of the Old Army (Demob), Kedrov's job was to seize Imperial Army materiél and facilities for the Bolsheviks' new Red Army. [6]

Artuzov admired and emulated his 41-year-old uncle Kedrov who in turn revered and imitated Cheka founder Dzerzhinsky, who likewise copied his boss Lenin. The four shared a ruthless mindset and the same absurdly self-conscious facial hair.

Artuzov

Kedrov

Dzerzhinsky

Lenin

The Goatee Men

<u>Arkhangelsk</u>

In March 1918, Artuzov, using his excellent German and a Swiss passport (perhaps his father's) with his birth surname Frauchi, chatted up some Swiss students in the Norwegian Embassy in St. Petersburg and learned that the famous jeweler Fabergé had hidden a trove of jewelry worth 1.6 million gold rubles (a bit less than a million dollars at the time, and many tens of millions of dollars in modern terms). Directed by his uncle Kedrov, Artuzov broke into the embassy and stole the jewelry that night, apparently with the help of at least one cousin, Bonifati Kedrov. Other embassies also were raided and pilfered, and various people arrested or shot. *[37, 115]*

A few months later, Artuzov went north with his uncle, a couple of cousins, and a special Red Army detachment of Latvian riflemen to "establish Soviet power" in the North. This special "Kedrov train" stopped on the way in Yaroslavl and Vologda to help "liquidate bandits and counter-revolutionaries" then reached the northern port of Arkhangelsk (Archangel). Using the train as lodging and base of operations, they killed traitors and seized tons of gold, warehouses of munitions, and mountains of coal. Control of the city would ebb and flow as Allied forces (British, French and American) moved into the city, fought the Bolsheviks in area battles, and withdrew by late 1919.

Artuzov and his uncle's group found themselves more or less in control of Arkhangelsk and the region. They arrested city officials, "eliminated unrest", and continued killing thousands of people who had not been sympathetic or actively loyal to the Bolsheviks. They also stole the food supplies of the island monastery Solovetsky (Solovki), a place to which we shall return.

The official and monumentally disingenuous <u>Great Soviet Encyclopedia</u> made innocuous note of Artuzov's Arkhangelsk labor: he "participated in the establishment of Soviet power in the North". It also gave him a suitably honorable but utterly false death date of July 1943, in the midst of the Great Patriotic War. *[73]*

After Arkhangelsk, Artuzov remained by his uncle's side during travels to Tambov and Baku, then built himself a career in the Cheka. He became head of counterintelligence but was demoted and later shot in the 1930s. Artuzov was replaced by stamp man Jan Olsky, who in due course was demoted to cafeteria manager and shot after a few years. Olsky was replaced by stamp man Nikolai Demidenko, who actually became the first of the stamp men to die. As we will see, when Demidenko's time at the wheel was up, he died of "illness" at a remarkably and suspiciously ideal moment and, thus, avoided the indignity of demotion and a bullet.

Chanel No. 5 and the Gulag

During and after the Russian Civil War, the city of Arkhangelsk, whose name and symbol were of a defender of good against evil, became both a nexus of horror and a womb that soon would yield two singular births, one sweeter-smelling than the other, but both born of spilled blood.

The city was founded where the Dvina River meets the White Sea, 120 miles south of the Arctic Circle and 250 miles east of the modern Russian-Finnish border. It is named for the Archangel Michael, one of the most important heavenly figures in Christianity, Judaism, and Islam—in each, he is a crucial defender of good against evil. It is an old city. The first recorded inhabitation is more than a thousand years ago. In the eleventh century, a monastery dedicated to Michael was built in the river's estuary. Several centuries later the nearby city was Arkhangelsk and grew into a significant trade and naval port.

When World War One's Allied forces (mostly British, American, and French) occupied the city and surroundings early in the Civil War, they imprisoned more than a thousand Bolsheviks in a concentration camp on Mudyug Island, a 27 mile boat ride into the river's estuary from the city center. Hundreds of prisoners died from hunger, cold, disease, and deliberate cruelty. Archived reports make clear that Mudyug was a terrible place. *[13]*

One of the camp commanders was an officer in the French forces in his late thirties named Ernest Beaux, who was of French descent but from Russia. Bolsheviks were anathema to Beaux—he had been on the board of directors of Russia's preeminent perfume company. The Revolution put an end to the business of selling scents to the aristocracy and forced Beaux's young family to flee Russia.

In his new role, Beaux interrogated Bolsheviks and sympathizers and imprisoned them on Mudyug. He authorized multiple transfers of typhus victims from the island to prison hospitals in Arkhangelsk, which led to an epidemic in the city. His reputation was sufficiently bad that a local Bolshevik newspaper Our War could exploit it with an article titled "The French Pig Bo", by one Nikandr Plastinin (whom we will meet as the first husband of Rebekka Plastinin, the Arkhangelsk lover/partner of Artuzov's uncle Kedrov).

Beaux claimed to have a remarkably sensitive nose—Mudyug's miasma must have left an indelible impression on him when he returned to France and the perfume trade. Despite his olfactory abilities, we can say that his memory proved breathtakingly selective.

Inspired (in his own words) by the crisp Russian air "beyond the Arctic Circle, at the time of the midnight sun, when the lakes and rivers release a perfume of extreme freshness", concentration camp officer Ernest Beaux returned to France where he gave birth to a new scent, the world's most famous fragrance—Chanel Number 5. [158]

Artuzov and his uncle Kedrov also knew of Mudyug. When they regained control of Arkhangelsk, it only reinforced their violent hatred of anti-Bolsheviks. [42, 43]

Soon, Artuzov would undertake his single most significant act in the distant North. Lenin and Dzherzhinsky telegraphed Kedrov, and Artuzov helped his uncle organize primitive concentration camps on the White Sea monastery islands of Solovetski (Solovki), the coastal village of Pertominsk, and the up-river village of Kholmogory and town of Shenkursk, places we will meet again.

All were a day or two by boat from Arkhangelsk and had Orthodox monastery-church complexes to serve as sturdy prison walls. The Solovki monastery closed in May 1920 and became a forced labor camp. Soon, countless thousands of people, some from the Arkhangelsk region, some from the 1920-1921 Tambov Rebellion, some from the 1921 Kronstadt Rebellion, and many from other parts of the Soviet Union, would enter these early camps. Some would survive, some would die.

One might die dragging enormous logs out of bitterly cold waters, or cutting trees in snow-covered swamps, or digging peat from a bog, or carrying stones, or harnessed to a plough.

One might die standing naked on a stump in a cloud of mosquitos, or shivering in an unheated punishment cell, or fighting over a piece of bread, or defecating uncontrollably during a typhoid epidemic, or being tied to a log and tossed down the hundreds of steps of Solovki's Sekirnaya Hill. And, of course, one might die from a bullet.

There were many ways to die.

Northern camp conditions were so bad that a 1922 investigative commission in Arkhangelsk took note. Artuzov and his uncle may have already left, but this is unclear, since the commission made notes about his uncle's wife Rebekka Plastinina. Some camp personnel were shot, and the senior ones (perhaps following Kedrov and his retinue) were transferred to southern Russia. [160, 166]

The Kholmogory site in particular is wrapped in incomprehensible irony. The village's name comes from the Finnish name Kalmomäki, which translates roughly as "corpse hill".

In the 1600s, Kholmogory developed a famous craft of elaborate carvings made from the ivory and bones of walrus, unearthed mammoth skeletons, and other creatures. The craft faded by the late 1800s but was revived in 1934 by decree of the Soviet Central Committee. Kholmogory bone carvings earned a gold medal at the 1937 International Exposition in Paris, and for decades the Soviet government handed out Kholmogory carvings as gifts to foreign dignitaries and diplomats. [161]

Women prisoners arriving at Solovki camp

Prisoners and guards, Solovki 1925

Since Kholmogory's ancient craft used locally-sourced bones, we can only wonder whether Stalin's reanimated carving industry ever used bones unearthed from the soil of Kholmogory's defunct death camp. If so, do any diplomatic gift collections around the world contain any Kholmogory carvings made from human bones? A private joke like this would have appealed to Stalin's sense of humor—there is an undocumented (and probably dubious) claim that at the Potsdam Conference in 1945 he served Churchill and Truman vodka distilled in Magadan, a city built entirely by prison labor.

In 1922-23 the Arkhangelsk-area camps initially established by Kedrov and Artuzov were re-organized. Kholmogory and Pertominsk were closed and any remaining prisoners were sent to the Solovetsky Islands, into the "Solovki [later Severnyy, or Northern] camp of special purpose forced labor", abbreviated SLON. Alexander Solzhenitsyn, never at a loss for words, called SLON the "Arctic Auschwitz". *[81, 82]*

SLON is the Russian word for elephant. When the camp (lager) was relabeled a prison (tyurma), the nickname changed to STON, the Russian word for groan.

Elephant or groan, it makes no real difference—Solovki was the "mother tumor" (another Solzhenitsyn phrase). The Arkhangelsk camps Artuzov and his uncle Kedrov created provided the methods and structure for a system of thousands of camps of labor and death which would swallow millions of people, all coordinated by a new Main Administration of Corrective Labor Camps (Glavnoe Upravlenie ispravitel'no-trudovykh LAGerei, better known by its obvious acronym).

Artur Artuzov and his uncle Mikhail Kedrov are, thus, co-founders of the entire Gulag.

Boris Gudz and Artuzov's last days

In the early and mid-1930s, Artuzov lost influence as his superiors fought for power. Near the end, his uncle Mikhail denounced him.

Boris Ignatievich Gudz, a friend of Artuzov who joined the Cheka, claimed Artuzov spent early 1937 working on a history of Soviet intelligence saying: "It's a necessary thing, and nobody will do it better than me." Gudz claimed to have two decades of Chekist service: escorting seized Ukrainian food to Moscow, erasing adversaries in Chechnya and on the Manchurian Railway, working in Japan, and helping his boss Artuzov. He also claimed stamp men Puzitsky and Syroezhkin tried to save Boris Savinkov from falling out a Lubyanka window in the Syndicate-2 operation.

Gudz remained unscathed, but his three sisters were not so lucky. *Alexandra Ignatievna Gudzya* was arrested and died in the notoriously deadly camp region Kolyma. *Maria* and *Galina* survived after exile in Turkmenistan. *[190, 191]*

Varlam Shalamov, a Gulag prisoner from 1929-1932, was Galina's husband. When his brother-in-law denounced him, Shalamov went to Kolyma for sixteen years. He survived to write one of the most famous Gulag books, Kolyma Tales. Shalamov died poor and lonely in 1982, more than two decades before the former brother-in-law who sent him to the camps. *[78]*

Gudz credited his own freedom to luck. Somehow he emerged as a Moscow bus driver in and after World War II. Born just after 1900, he lived into the twenty-first century and died at age 104 or 105.

In various late-life interviews he focused on Artuzov, the Cheka, and himself. Occasionally he referred to his sister Alexandra as a victim, but he did not mention his former brother-in-law or his exiled sisters.

Gudz's niece-in-law, Svetlana Ivanovna Zlobina, says Gudz angered his father with his actions, skipped his father's funeral, lied about his role (e.g. being a Tokyo embassy driver, not a spymaster), and was secretive and insincere. *[74, 75, 77, 78, 191]*

Gudz's version of Artuzov's last work as official historian is not credible. According to a much more believable account, Artuzov spent his last days rummaging through archives to untangle a complex, imaginary internal conspiracy which he submitted to new NKVD chief Nikolai Yezhov in hope of saving his own skin. *[70]*

Whether working on historical preservation or a paper lifesaver, Artuzov failed. Arrested in his office on 13 May 1937, interrogators persuaded him by 27 May to agree that "further resistance was useless", and he began confessing to treason. After three months, he wound up as number 38 on the 20 August 1937 "arrest and kill" list of former NKVD employees. Sometime after midnight, Artur Frauchi, the cheesemaker's son and one-time metallurgist, was convicted and shot. *[21, 23]*

Cremated at the Donskoye cemetery, he was the first stamp man dumped in Donskoye's large pit for the ashes of executed prisoners, Common Grave Number 1 (Общая могила № 1).

Donskoye is where the Soviets built Moscow's first crematorium in the late 1920s. They installed two modern crematory ovens made in Germany. When the crematorium was finished and tested, the performance of the ovens was deemed very "satisfactory". Perhaps further research might reveal whether the same manufacturer later supplied any ovens to the Third Reich's concentration camps.

Cousins

For Artuzov, the Cheka was an extended family affair. We can explore it in detail. His maternal aunt, Olga Avgustovna Didrikil was his uncle Mikhail's first wife. It appears they had four children.

Silva Kedrova, or Silvia, is referenced as a student who reminisced about her father and his expectation that his children should read extensively. Apparently born in 1919, she was the youngest of Mikhail Kedrov's four children. *[115]*

Bonifati Kedrov (1903-1985) started early at age 14 or 15, according to an official Kedrov book, by helping his father break into foreign embassy buildings to seize anti-Bolsheviks hiding in Petrograd. Presumably these prisoners were liquidated in Chekist fashion. It seems he also helped his cousin Artur steal jewelry from the Swiss embassy as mentioned earlier. Later, Bonifati went with his father and cousin to the Tambov region to kill rebellious peasants, then to Baku to requisition fish. *[115]*

Bonifati became a Chekist in a chemistry professor's clothing. He espoused his father's pro-Bolshevik, pro-Stalinist views throughout life, most notably in mid-career when he publicly ruined chemists and physicists who worked with "Western" scientific theories and research. He even wrote a children's textbook explaining how true science is Marxist-Leninist. *[47, 48]*

Yuri Kedrov (1905 - ?) was a mysterious youth who might have started early as well. A year and a half younger than Bonifati, Yuri was mentioned as being an orderly for his father in 1918 and helping Chekists to chop wood outside Moscow in late 1919. Perhaps his father made him do this—it certainly does not sound like much fun for a fourteen-year-old. *[115]*

There are no references to Yuri's whereabouts after 1919. His surviving brother Bonifati provided no public clues. One source hints that he killed himself as a teenager. As we will see, if he rode the rails with his father Mikhail to Arkhangelsk and other places, and saw what happened there, suicide would be unsurprising.

Igor Mikhailovich Kedrov (1908-1940) worked in the Cheka for two decades. In the 1936-1938 surge of arrests and executions under NKVD secret police chief Nikolai Yezhov, he earned a reputation as "one of the most vicious of the interrogators." *[44]*

In mid-1938, Lavrenty Beria became Yezhov's deputy as a precursor to replacing him. Igor's father had tried to discredit Beria in Azerbaijan back in 1921-22 and knew that the notoriously unforgiving Beria would seek revenge. He attempted to preempt this by using Igor to write a letter to Stalin criticizing Beria.

It was a stunning miscalculation. By the end of 1938, Yezhov was out, demoted to commissar of water transport, and Beria was in charge of the NKVD. His revenge was swift. Igor was arrested on 20 February 1939 and held in prison for nearly a year. Number 130 on the 16 January 1940 kill list, Igor was convicted on the 24th, shot on the 25th, and cremated at the Donskoye cemetery, his ashes dumped in with those of his cousin Artuzov in Common Grave Number 1.

Igor had a wife, Raisa Fedorovna Melikhova (or Kedrova) and three children, Artem, Boris, and Natalya. Raisa was left in the dark for a long time—in the 1953 case against Beria, Raisa stated that she was told in April 1941 that Igor's sentence was ten years in prison without the right of correspondence.

The 1953 Beria file also refers to Igor's August 1939 farewell letter from prison to his son Temochka (Artem). The letter was withheld—Raisa received it from the investigator fourteen years later. Igor tells his son to read Robinson Crusoe, Tom Sawyer, and The Odyssey. It is interesting to ponder Igor's motives for these book choices. *[21, 57]*

Johann Friedrichovich Tubala (1896-1938), sometimes denoted Ivan or Iogan Fedorovich, was a cousin of sorts. The son of close family friends from Estonia, he went north to Arkhangelsk with Mikhail Kedrov, then south with him, Bonifati, and Artuzov to Tambov and Baku, where he was involved in Kedrov's efforts to undermine Lavrenty Beria's role in Azerbaijan and Georgia. Later he became a Gulag camp officer. Arrested on 19 October 1937 in Tbilisi, he spent eight months in prison, apparently in Tbilisi. Number 154 on the 10 June 1938 kill list, he was convicted 21 June and shot the next day. His wife Elyanora Ignatievna Tubala remained in the city. Number 218 on the kill list for 12 September 1938, she was arrested 11 October and shot two days later. *[21, 122, 123]*

Elyanora was not Tubala's first wife—he was previously married to Artur Artuzov's sister Vera Frauchi, with whom he had several children. One benefit of the divorce for Vera was that she and her children were not arrested, exiled, sent to the camps, or shot.

Artuzov and/or his cousins are likely in this photo in Arkhangelsk from a 1988 anthology about Mikhail Kedrov. It looks like a family photo, a father with sons or nephews on the side deck of a boat. We can see the captain at the rear and angled rigging on the left. Perhaps they are on their way to or from the dark sites of Mudyug, Solovki, Pertominsk, or Kholomogory.

Mikhail Kedrov with Chekists (some may be relatives)
Arkhangelsk, dated as 1920 [115]

Obvious candidates for relatives are the three boys or young men in the front. The two young men immediately behind Kedrov are possibilities, too.

At the time, Igor would have been 11-12 years old, Yuri 14-15, and Bonifati 16-17. Nephew Artur would have been 28 or 29, and foster-son Johann 23 or 24.

Although the individuals in the photo are uncertain, we do know that Kedrov took at least three family members to Arkhangelsk: his nephew Artur, his son Bonifati, and his foster-son Johann Tubala. Yuri and Igor were younger but may have gone, too.

Uncle Mikhail

Mikhail Sergeevich Kedrov (28 Feb 1878 – 28 Oct/1Nov 1941) took Artuzov and other young relatives to Arkhangelsk. Before and after, his famous train cars rolled along various fronts in the Civil War, bringing executions and control. He was a committed Bolshevik known for his musicality, violence, and mental instability.

He also was a printer and writer dedicated to the Marxist-Leninist cause. He went to prison for sedition and bomb-making. Around 1902 he opened Zerno Publishing in St. Petersburg to print subversive literature by Lenin and others.

He moved to Switzerland and studied medicine, met his hero Lenin in Bern, and the two became closely connected. Around 1916 he returned to Russia and worked as a doctor. As the Revolution unfolded, he was appointed to run investigative commissions in Moscow, St. Petersburg and other cities to root out non-enthusiasts, seize Russian Army supplies for the Bolsheviks, confiscate guns, force civilian doctors and nurses into conscription for work at the battlefront, and so on. His son Bonifati's memoirs overlooked these activities but recalled in detail how Kedrov used his medical training to fight typhoid epidemics in the cities he visited.

In mid-1918 he left for the north. He stopped in Yaroslavl to "clear foreign elements" but didn't stay long. The city became a major civil war battleground and was mostly destroyed. In one estimate, by late 1918 the city's population had dropped from 128,000 to about 76,000. Some were killed in battle, many had fled, and the Cheka busied itself with executions. *[164]*

Kedrov then stopped in Vologda. The provincial and city governments were "finally liquidated" and replaced by new Bolshevik administrators. A detachment stole food and church valuables from a convent in Veliky Ustyug while Kedrov looted Vologda banks.

Coincidentally, Vologda was the home of young Varlam Shalamov, the writer whom Artuzov's assistant Boris Gudz would later denounce. Shalamov was only twelve when Kedrov arrived, but his memoirs The Fourth Vologda bitterly condemn Kedrov's arrests and killings in Vologda. Adolescent Shalamov could not possibly have imagined at the time that Kedrov's nephew's friend Gudz would become his brother-in-law who would be responsible for Shalamov's sixteen years in Kolyma camps.

Kedrov applied his Swiss training and ordered the city to empty out cesspools and clean up garbage or suffer fines and punishments. Complying with this medical edict was difficult for residents—the Bolsheviks were stealing or eating all the city's cart-pulling draft horses. Thousands of Red Army soldiers added to the supply of sewage and garbage, and Vologda soon "plunged into the abyss of a communal catastrophe" of typhoid epidemics. *[115, 164, 165]*

Vologda would have to sort out sanitation on its own. Kedrov moved onward to Arkhangelsk in early June to issue new edicts blaming entrepreneurs for lumber industry sabotage and speculators for food shortages. He "worked around the clock" with a "firm Bolshevik hand" and "all necessary measures" to repress uprisings, impose martial law, and "liquidate" the existing government. To empty out the city's enormous cache of ammunition and coal, he "mobilized the entire population" (i.e., forced people) to load it onto trains and boats. His commission announced large-scale military conscription into the Red Army. This sparked more rebellions and temporary occupation by the Allies' foreign forces. When the Allies left, things calmed down thanks to Kedrov's contingent of Latvian machine-gunners and the arrival of new weapons from Moscow. *[115]*

Afterward, Kedrov rode the rails with his young relatives to the Tambov region to support the Red Army with stamp man Grigory Syroezhkin and other Chekists. Eventually more than 100,000 local peasants would be killed in the 1920-1921 Tambov Rebellion.

As the great 1920s Soviet famine grew, Kedrov went further south in 1921 to the Caspian Sea and all the way to Azerbaijan and Georgia, to reinforce Soviet rule and to requisition (seize) food. Suspicious of foreign relief agencies, he held trainloads of fish for a while before releasing it to the starving Samara region. He also confiscated rice from farmers and from ships operated by "smugglers". *[115]*

In Baku, Kedrov crossed paths with Lavrenty Beria, who was involved with the Azeri Cheka. Kedrov's failed attempt to undermine Beria's local authority would spell Kedrov's demise two decades later.

Kedrov's murderous time in the North was studied by the 1922 investigative commission. Numerous complaints included a citizen's letter sent directly to Lenin with the probably exaggerated claim that Kedrov executed more than 7,000 prisoners. *[161, p. 41]*

Kedrov's longtime association with Lenin saved him. Some sources claim he was put in a mental institution. A more likely path was internal exile, as we can deduce from essays which detail his relocation to remote Ust-Tsilma, several hundred miles east of Arkhangelsk, where he provided Soviet freedom to the hapless locals. He wrote plans for regional development, forced native trappers to sell their furs (a valuable export) only to the government, worked on shipping plans for the Pechora River, and raised "cultural life" by publishing a new Soviet newspaper. After a year and a half of this redemptive work, he returned to Moscow in late 1923. *[115]*

Kedrov liked to write. In 1927 he published a memoir about Arkhangelsk and in 1930 a set of essays about the port of Murmansk in the civil war. His last books, in 1932, were a co-authored French-language book on Lenin and a book (printed in multiple countries) about printing Lenin's writings. *[108, 109, 129, 132, 130]*

Kedrov was arrested in April 1939, two months after Igor. His son Bonifati says the date was 16 April 1939. Kedrov was number 184 on the 6 September 1940 list of arrests for anti-Soviet activities. A 1989 <u>Pravda</u> article claimed he was tried and, most unusually, acquitted on 9 July 1941, barely two weeks after the start of the German invasion. Presumably the court had new things to worry about.

This acquittal is consistent with prosecution records in the 1953 investigation into Beria. Kedrov had compromising material on Beria from early times in Baku, according to his daughter-in-law Raisa. Beria used his acolyte Vsevelod Merkulov to try to reverse the acquittal, but on 30 August the court refused. *[21, 153, 157, 170, 171]*

Beria ignored the court and kept Kedrov in prison anyway. Soon the Germans neared Moscow and on 18 October 1941 Beria listed twenty-five inmates to be shipped east and shot. Kedrov, now age 63, was the last name added (number 25). Most were shot on the 28th in Barbysh, a suburb of Kuibyshev (now Samara). Kedrov and four others may have been shot three days later on 1 November, either in Barbysh or possibly Saratov, almost three hundred miles from Kuibyshev. Beria made procurator general Bochkov back-date and sign an order authorizing the "legality" of the executions. *[233]*

The Kedrovs became more famous after death. Both Mikhail and Igor Kedrov's arrests and executions were important elements used to develop the factual criminal case against Beria in 1953. Several years later, Khrushchev's famous 1956 "Secret Speech" used a prison letter from Kedrov as evidence to denounce Stalin.

The <u>Great Soviet Encyclopedia</u> praises Kedrov but omits his work in Arkhangelsk and the circumstances of his death, and misstates his date of death. *[45, 46, 73]*

Throughout life, Kedrov sported the goatee his nephew so admired and copied.

Mikhail Kedrov, dated as 1936 [115]

Should we wonder about Kedrov's feelings at the end? His nephew, niece-in-law, another nephew, a foster son and his wife's ex-husband were all arrested and shot. After his own son Igor was shot, Kedrov waited almost two years for his own bullet. Did he mourn the deaths of his young relatives? Did he feel remorse for setting the Gulag system in motion? His Swiss medical education had offered a different path—did he regret not taking it?

Modern historian Sergei Bilokin doubts Kedrov was haunted by his victims' ghosts. *[159]*

It is difficult to know Kedrov's feelings, or to care. The only record we have of his prison time is his written complaints about his innocence, loyal service, and undeserved suffering.

Aunt Rebekka

Rebekka Akibovna Meisel (or Maisel), better known as Rebekka Plastinina, became Kedrov's co-worker, lover and second wife when he came with his nephew Artuzov to Arkhangelsk. Her story reveals a lot about the early world of the stamp men.

Rebekka was born in 1886 to Akiba Maisel, a notary or lawyer, and his wife Olga (Palkina) in the heavily Jewish city of Grodno, on the border of western Belarus-eastern Poland. By her early twenties she had moved to Paris.

Nikandr Fedorovich Plastinin, her first husband, was from Padenga village by Shenkursk, the site of a 1919 bloody Bolshevik-Allies battle and a hundred miles southeast (upriver) of Arkhangelsk.

We don't know whether Rebekka's family was patriarchal and traditional or the type to raise her as a well-educated modern woman. It is hard to imagine that her parents would have been especially happy with their daughter joining a Russian revolutionary from sub-Arctic Russia. Using a different lens, though, we can speculate that they might have been pleased for her to begin a twentieth-century life in France with the bookish son of a Russian merchant.

It seems they may have met in St. Petersburg. Russia forcibly moved many Jews eastward from her hometown of Grodno, and her parents died in St. Petersburg sometime during World War I.

One version says Rebekka helped Nikandr in revolutionary activities and that they spent years in exile in Paris, where Nikandr took on various jobs, even cleaning shop windows at night. Certainly, life was difficult for many foreign-born residents of the city. *[174]*

Pre-war Paris had many Russian émigrés, both pro and anti-Tsarist. Eventually the young family moved to Switzerland to join Lenin and others, like Mikhail Kedrov and Anna Driesenstock, whom Rebekka and Nikandr would later re-marry.

They returned to Russia, possibly with Lenin to St. Petersburg, and headed north to Shenkursk, where Nikandr began writing for the town's newspaper, which still recalls him as a prolific contributor. He also wrote propaganda for the regional Red Army paper Our War (Наша война) with fiery titles like "The hero and the bastard", "Go on, take a bite!!", and the previously mentioned "French pig" article about the Mudyug camp officer Ernest Beaux. Incendiary language with the righteousness of youth came easily to Nikandr. *[105, 106]*

There are three publicly-known photos of Rebekka. The first is a family portrait in Switzerland—a high-quality studio photo of a stylish young family.

Nikandr Plastinin, Rebekka Meisel & son Vladimir
Switzerland, 1916

In her second photo, Rebekka stands to the side of a Shenkursk Bolshevik group. The photo probably is from spring of 1919 since the Red Army had pushed out the foreign Allied forces in January. The winter snow has melted—men's shoes and Rebekka's coattails are spattered with mud. Her stylish hat and coat mark her as an outsider, and she seems to have no warm link to the group.

Nikandr Plastinin (arms crossed) and Rebekka Meisel (far right)
with Bolshevik group in Shenkursk, probably spring 1919

Her husband Nikandr is in the photo, too. The seated man with light-colored clothing and no hat has Nikandr's small build and the same shoulders, ears, eyebrows, and hairline. Arms crossed, he stares into the distance, away from Rebekka and the camera. We should not be surprised that he appears tense—unexpected plot twists in the Bolshevik revolution were tearing his families apart.

His wife was preparing to leave him and would take their son. His Shenkursk family was shattered by his "Bolshevik maximalism". We can assume that his family's money probably helped him to move to

France and Switzerland and avoid the brunt of World War I. When Nikandr came home he wrote propaganda for a violent political movement which defined his parents and relatives as class enemies.

Nikandr's little sister Vera was already traumatized—the previous summer in July 1918 her husband Yakov Petrovich Levanidov was seized by her brother's beloved Bolsheviks. Yakov never returned. More than seven decades later, family descendants learned he had been shot and thrown into the Dvina River in September. *[167]*

In modern lists, there are a variety of Shenkurst and Arkhangelsk Plastinins who in the '20s and '30s were sent to the camps or shot.

Rebekka's third photo must be from the mid-to-late 1920s. Her youthful attractiveness and French fashion are long gone, traded for coarse Bolshevik looks. Husband Nikandr is out of the picture as well, replaced by Mikhail Kedrov. Some sources misidentify the boy as Kedrov's son Igor. Compare the light eyes, wide ears, small mouth and distinctive chin to the 1916 photo—the young man is Rebekka's son Vladimir, now on his way to a Chekist career.

Chekist family:
Rebekka Meisel, son Vladimir Plastinin, and Mikhail Kedrov

Maybe Rebekka was the prototypical hard Bolshevik, or just young and foolish. Perhaps she moved from Switzerland to the distant forests of northern Russia with fierce political beliefs, or to seek her family in St. Petersburg, or for fear she and her child would be abandoned. She had seen years of freedom and modernity in the West—it is curious to imagine she was happy to trade that away. Maybe she went with enthusiasm for revolution against the rotten Tsarists, or hope of seeing Mikhail Kedrov again, or with fear.

Rebekka joined Kedrov's commission to subdue and deplete the city. Graphic accounts claim she was a ruthless judge and killer like Kedrov, but these are unverified and overdone. For example, Bromage's lurid biography of Dzerzhinsky claims Rebekka killed all of Plastinin's relatives, drowned five hundred officers on a barge, shot 120 people in a row, and knifed and flogged others: "She was a strong woman, with an arm of steel." Later, a government commission noted a "sick and nervous" demeanor in Plastinina but did not explain. She then moved with Kedrov to remote Ust-Tsilma and helped him start his newspaper there. *[115, 156, 160, 192]*

Rebekka seems to have been emotionally damaged. Maybe she was a submissive woman, debased by Nikandr and Kedrov, who took out her pain on others. Zealous physical cruelty is not exclusive to men, but it is less common in women. Or, maybe she really was a dyed-in-the-wool Bolshevik. We can only speculate.

Nikandr Plastinin lost his dapper style, his wife, and his son. He continued for years as a propaganda writer in various cities, and may have worked in the Soviet embassy in Athens, Greece with his new wife, Chekist and propagandist **Anna Mironovna Dreizenshtok**, whom he knew from Switzerland. They moved to the far eastern village of Borzya (Borzinsky district, Chita region). In 1937 Anna was arrested and released, but Nikandr's personal conflicts with co-workers in railway police work doomed him. [227, 228, 229]

He was sent to Nizhneudinsk camp (Taishet region, Irkutsk), a bleak rail stop almost three thousand miles from his hometown. Many prisoners there simply froze or starved to death. [110]

Thousands of prisoners were shipped to the Taishet region area in the winter of 1937-38 to work on a new rail line. Perhaps this was Nikandr's final role in building the radiant Soviet future. He seems to have died of unspecified causes on 19 May 1938. [58, 62]

Vladimir Nikandrovich Plastinin was born to Rebekka and Nikandr in 1909 in Paris. He later wrote that he met his future step-father Kedrov when he was ten. We do not know if he went to Ust-Tsilma with his mother and Kedrov, but he did grow up to join his step-father in the Cheka/OGPU. Vladimir was promoted to a lieutenant on 28 May 1938, nine days after his father Nikandr died in a Gulag camp. He was arrested and dismissed on 1 July 1939, but survived. At some point before or after his arrest he married one Alevtina Kozminichna Nikitina. Later he married an unidentified woman—perhaps Alevtina divorced him for political reasons.

On the present-day genealogy website *geni.com*, the public entry for Vladimir's ex-wife Alevtina conceals a child's name. Vladimir's own public entry conceals names of his second wife and multiple children. Only one son is publicly identified: Mikhail Vladimirovich Plastinin. Exploring this might lead into our present. [59, 60, 63]

By the early 1950s Vladimir was in Voronezh, Russia. He died in 1973, a lifetime away from his childhood in France and Switzerland.

As for Rebekka, her fate is unclear. Alexander Solzhenitsyn claimed she was on the Supreme Court of the Russian Republic in the early 1940s and died in October 1946, but provides no evidence.

Rebekka's stepson Bonifati Kedrov made the same claim in paperwork when seeking his father's political rehabilitation in 1953 but was uncertain if it was a Russian or Soviet court.

Perhaps the claim was a confused derivation of her fate. She was alive after 16 April 1939 (Bonifati recounted her detailed story of his father's arrest), but then her trail goes cold. *[104, 153]*

It is possible that she worked in the court system before her husband's arrest. The Supreme Court of the USSR was comprised of numerous departments. Under Stalin the court was impotent, and during the war it had even less to do. By 1949 the court had several hundred employees; fewer than one hundred were judges.

Gaining a job in the courts after Kedrov was arrested seems unlikely but given the occasional absurdity of Soviet processes and the administrative chaos of wartime Moscow, nothing is impossible.

In fact, though, there were plenty of reasons to arrest and kill or exile her. Both her husbands had been arrested and she was an Old Bolshevik with a bad reputation from Arkhangelsk.

It would have been easy to denounce her as a spy. She was a foreigner with an accent—western Belarusian, eastern Polish, Yiddish, or German, depending on how she was raised in Grodno. She had lived for years in capitalist Western Europe. All this, combined with her Jewish ethnicity, would have made her an easy mark as a "rootless cosmopolitan", one of Stalin's coded epithets for Jews.

Rebekka's sister Anna joined her in Moscow in the 1920s (and has modern descendants). The modern genealogy website *geni.com* says her older brother doctor Moses Akibovich Meisel (1879-1942) and his son Sergei Moiseevich Meisel died in January 1942 during the siege of Leningrad, in which more than one million residents would die of hunger, disease, and cold. Leningrad's temperature that January reached 40 degrees below zero.

Rebekka had another brother, Yakov Akibovich. US National Archives and Ellis Island databases identify various Yakov Meisels with alternative spellings, including one Jacob Meizel, age 16, from Russia, traveling in steerage on the ship Michigan from Liverpool, who arrived 21 January 1891. This could be Rebekka's brother, since one source states he moved to the United States in the 1890s. *[176]*

Perhaps Rebekka used Kedrov's acquittal to retain or obtain employment. Allies were scarce for anyone in the toxic Moscow environment. It is not clear if her sister Anna had any influence. Her strongest ally would have been her son Vladimir, but he was arrested then released at an unknown date. The Kedrov, Plastinin, or Frautchi families would have mixed feelings about her, and returning to Western Europe was by now impossible. Her family was gone from her childhood home of Grodno on the old Polish-Belarusian border, and that city would soon be savaged by German forces seeking to exterminate Jews, Communists, Poles, and Belarusians. Later, Soviet forces would over-run Grodno's rubble and kill many of the starved survivors as suspected collaborators.

One part of the tale is believable and potentially verifiable—the claim that she was buried in Moscow's Donskoye Cemetery. If she was executed after Kedrov's arrest, she might be with her stepson Igor Kedrov and his cousin Artuzov in the prisoner ash pit known as Common Grave Number 1, since it was used until 1942. However, she is not on the list of executed prisoners cremated at Donskoye.

Alternatively, if she did avoid arrest and execution, she may be in Donskoye's huge ash urn columbarium. Further research might shed light. There does not seem to be a readily available comprehensive list or photographic index of the thousands of ash receptacles, and she is not listed in a directory of the cemetery's regular graves. *[107]*

Artuzov's own family

Let us return now to our first stamp man, Artur Artuzov. Even for a senior Chekist, life was not easy. Compare Artuzov's well-kempt youth with the later gaunter, shoeless family brood.

Artuzov (at far left), Frauchi family and friends, after 1900

Artuzov (leftward rear, with beard) and extended family 1925

When Artur Artuzov was shot, his immediate family fell into the floodwaters as well. *[50, 53, 54]*

His father died in the early 1920s, likely of natural causes. His mother died in 1938 amidst her children's arrests and executions.

Artuzov's brother **Rudolf Frauchi**, was arrested 23 March 1938 and shot on 9 August at the Butovo shooting grounds outside Moscow, where 20,000-plus people were executed in less than two years. Brother **Viktor Frauchi** was investigated, moved five hundred miles east to Kazan, and lived until 1986. Sister **Evgenia Frauchi** was investigated and survived. Sister **Vera Frauchi**, noted earlier as the ex-wife of Johann Tubala, survived. Sister **Nina Frauchi** survived, too, although she divorced her husband **Georgy Fedorovich Kolontay** (Kolontaev), who was arrested in 1937 a month after his brother-in-law Artuzov was shot. He survived his eight years in Kolyma camps.

Artuzov's first wife, **Lidia Dmitrievna Slugina**, married him in 1918. They divorced in 1935, but it is not clear what happened to her. They had three children: **Lidia Frauchi** married to become Lidia Arturovna Stempkovskaya and **Eleonora Frauchi** married to become Eleonora Arturovna Denurova. Their son Kamill was sent to the Kolyma camps and survived.

Artuzov's second wife, **Inna Mihailovna** had two previous husbands: **Ivan (Janis) Mezhlauk** (shot April 1938) and **Grigory Tylis** (shot October 1937, sometimes described as Lidia's husbands. Inna supposedly had a spinal problem that required treatment in France—and thus a travel permit. Artuzov is said to have asked Nikolai Yezhov, the young Central Committee apparatchik in charge of such things before he became NKVD chief, and received the needed permit (twice, it seems). If the story is true, maybe it was an attempt to explore refuge—by 1936 Artuzov had to know that time was running out for senior Chekists. *[61]*

Inna was arrested on 28 May 1937, two weeks after her husband. Exactly one year after her husband's name was put on the kill list, Inna landed as number 2 on the 20 August 1938 kill list as the wife of an enemy of the people, and was promptly shot on the 26th. *[53, 21]*

Artuzov probably sensed what was coming. Family photos one day in the mid-1930s show him with children Nora (Eleonora) and Kamill soon before his demise. More than just formally posed, the pictures seem stiff, even tense.

Artuzov and daughter Nora, possibly 1936

Artuzov and son Kamill (one photo re-touched) possibly 1936

Kamill in camp

Kamill was only 14 or 15 when his father and step-mother were shot. As the "son of an enemy of the people" he was arrested and sent to terrifyingly remote and cold Kolyma, where prisoners often died after only one or two months of logging or mining. Summer in the land of the midnight sun meant endless workdays in clouds of mosquitos. In winter's perpetual dark and gloom, outdoor work would be if the thermometer fell to -55 degrees, but camp commanders read the gauge so this rarely happened. Regardless of the season, a frightened teenager could not fight or scheme for survival. Varlam Shalamov (the brother-in-law of Boris Gudz, friend of Kamill's father) called Kolyma "Auschwitz without the ovens".

Kamill did not last long. Soon he was put in a *zemlyanka* (a primitive covered dugout house) for "goners": the *dokhodyagi*, the quasi-living skeletons no longer capable of any work who were stored until they died. The boy lived only because camp administration panicked when suddenly ordered from above to have a music band. Someone remembered a young goner was said to have played violin. When they pulled him out to restore him, he was so weak that he could eat only one or two spoons of kasha (oatmeal) at a time. [49, 51]

With that rare luck, and with the safer surname Frautschi, Kamill sought refuge in beauty—he became a revered guitarist and teacher. We hear his independence, regarding musical rules at least, in the 2008 documentary <u>Frautschi</u>: "There are no authorities. None." [52]

Kamill died on 21 August 1997, sixty years to the day after his father was shot, and five days short of fifty-nine years after his step-mother Inna was shot.

Nikolai Ivanovich Demidenko

1 January 1896 - 26 June 1934
Kidnapper

Ukrainian Demidenko began in Red Army tribunals and the Kiev police. Dzerzhinsky sent him in 1921 to "catch agents and spies" as the Soviets invaded the tiny but newly free country of Georgia. *[9]*

As usual, the Cheka used terror. It is said that in one week in 1924 Chekist agents killed more than 12,000 Georgians. Even if this number is exaggerated, Georgian sources stress the indiscriminate nature of Chekist terror. Afterward, the Soviet government imposed a heavy hand on writers, artists, peasants, politicians, and clergy in Stalin's and Beria's home country. A Soviet office monolith replaced Tbilisi's largest cathedral. The main square was renamed for Beria, then Lenin. Now it is Freedom Square. Lenin's statue has been torn down and replaced with Saint George slaying the dragon. The nation's patron saint faces north, toward Russia.

By 1922 Demidenko was stamp man Artuzov's assistant. In Operation Syndicate-2, he and stamp man Puzitsky helped lure expatriate Boris Savinkov to Russia for interrogation and execution. [54]

Demidenko soon received the highest Soviet honor. A 1926 directory lists "Demidenko, N.K., OGPU worker" as a 1924 recipient of the Order of the Red Banner. [4]

In 1930 he and agents dressed as French policemen went to Paris for a daylight street attack and kidnapped Russian exile Alexander Kutepov, ostensibly for return to Moscow. The victim never reappeared—Demidenko may have killed him in Paris and disposed of the body. The project was organized by stamp man Puzitsky. [72]

By 1934, Demidenko was in Moscow as head of the OGPU's counterintelligence department; he replaced stamp man Jan Olsky who had replaced stamp man Artuzov. Their patron Felix Dzerzhinsky died in 1926 (probably by poison) and was replaced by his deputy Vyacheslav Menzhinsky, who died only several weeks before Demidenko and was replaced by his deputy Genrikh Yagoda.

Officially, Demidenko died of illness at age 38, on 26 June 1934. More likely, he was murdered. Several days later, the OGPU was merged into the new NKVD headed by Genrikh Yagoda, who was busy replacing OGPU officials with his own loyalists. Yagoda, an expert in poison, later confessed to killing Menzhinsky. It is very likely that he killed Demidenko as well as part of his takeover.

In the late 1920s and early 1930s, Demidenko was centrally involved in collectivizing agriculture. Farmers who resisted were exiled, arrested, or killed. In practice, such farmers (labeled *kulak*s, or "fists") ranged from landowners with tenants to impoverished peasants with one cow. Stalin's open letter "On the elimination of the kulaks as a class", stated without ambiguity that the kulak class was to be "smashed in open battle and...*deprived* of the productive sources of its existence". Stalin emphasized "deprived" in the original... *[134]*

By June 1931 Demidenko was well aware of logistical difficulties, local "excesses", and social and agricultural problems of collectivization, deportation, and the kulak class elimination effort, as shown by his lengthy communications with his outlying OGPU offices to gain information and to direct operational activities. *[135, 136]*

Collectivization was supposed to re-shape society, reduce dissent, spur agriculture, and support industrialization. Demidenko had seen firsthand and in intimate detail that this showpiece Soviet policy was an inefficient and deadly mess. In following years, the government would continually seek to contain the damage, conceal the evidence, and depict collectivization as a historically unique success.

Of course, people do die of illness, and Soviet medicine in the early 1930s was not very good, even for high-ranking Chekists in Moscow. Still, Demidenko was a department chief in an agency that was being taken over by a new agency. He belonged to a cadre of long-time senior colleagues who would be killed in the next several years. Since he died at a suspiciously ideal moment, we can infer that he most likely was murdered. He was the first of his group to die.

Artamonov's remarkable catalog (1995, p. 104) lists him in section 23 of Moscow's Vagankovskoe Cemetery. Indeed, the grave exists. The base of his memorial column has an engraved epitaph "Honorable Chekist of the Red Banner Nikolai Demidenko 1896-1934." A note below the epitaph, "Kolenka no one will ever replace you to us. Olga, Katya", is done in relief carving and appears to have been added later. Kolenka is a diminutive of endearment for Nikolai, so the note clearly is intended to come from his family, although we do not know who actually added it. A small gravestone for Ekaterina (Katya) Demidenko is next to his. *[7, 39, 107]*

Jan Kalikstovich Olsky (Kulikovsky)

22 December 1898 - 27 November 1937
Rebellion crusher

Today, in Belarus, the national secret police, still named the **KGB**, give Olsky a rather positive official biography as an early chief. [2]

Jan Kalikstovich Kulikovsky was born in the Russian Empire's Lithuania region. He became Olsky to hide his Polish ethnicity so it would not adversely affect him when he volunteered for "Soviet work" in Vilnius (the capital of modern Lithuania). [183]

In 1919, he assessed a **Red Army** unit and "liquidated" almost sixty "Polish" spies. He soon joined the Cheka's elite—by June 1921, at age 22, Olsky was head of the Belarus Cheka. He led "punitive" efforts to "crush" and "eliminate" thousands of enemies of Soviet power. In the next thirty years, hundreds of thousands of Belarusians would be swept away by the Cheka, some killed, most exiled. [1, 2]

By 1923, Olsky returned to Moscow to head an **OGPU** counterintelligence division; he reported to Demidenko and Artuzov.

By 1926 he was head of the "Special Department", the OGPU's internal surveillance and enforcement division. One of his office's tasks was to investigate problems in aircraft production. The problems were real enough (quality, quantity, delays and so on) but they were evidence of larger problems endemic to the entire Soviet Union—shortages, poor coordination, conflicting incentives and disincentives, rushed industrialization, improper design and production, improper equipment and training, and the list goes on.

Olsky was a bright young man. He realized that actual problems which could not be solved were not administratively palatable problems. Thus, his "analysis" of aircraft production problems alleged sabotage and willful disobedience of his unit's orders. *[137]*

By 1930, the USSR was in its first 5-Year-Plan. Farms were being collectivized and grain was being exported to buy foreign industrial equipment. Olsky and stamp man Puzitsky enforced the mass exile of hundreds of thousands of angry peasants. They seized crops and sent the hapless farmers to remote ends of the Soviet Union. *[26]*

Olsky became chief of counterintelligence (KRO) when Artuzov was transferred out. Stamp men Demidenko, Puzitsky, and Styrne now reported to Olsky. Demidenko would later replace him.

As KRO chief, he had a heavy load of exile problems. Some exiles escaped their new settlements, returned home, and talked about their suffering in exile. The OGPU was expected to meet and exceed arbitrary numerical arrest goals without violating procedural requirements, but the rules for selecting, provisioning, transporting, and resettling exiles frequently conflicted with reality. The OGPU couldn't find enough food for those staying behind, let alone the deportees, and reports of cannibalism became more common. Field offices were ordered to meet impossible standards for equipping deportees to survive. The archives contain an exhausting stream of reports to and edicts from his offices regarding conflicting and unsolvable problems. *[138, 139, 141, 142, 143]*

Chekists confiscate grain hidden by peasants

As collectivization unfolded, so did bureaucratic infighting. Olsky was demoted and sent to manage Moscow's government cafeterias.

The December 1934 murder of Leningrad party-chief Sergei Kirov conveniently shifted national conversation and debate (what was left of it, anyway) from the aftermath of collectivization to the dangers of spies and sabotage. Unfortunately for cafeteria chief Olsky, he criticized the new secret police chief Genrikh Yagoda for investigative incompetence in the Kirov investigation (Olsky was friends with Filip Medved, one of the people blamed for Kirov's death). Olsky failed to grasp that Kirov was killed by Yagoda on Stalin's orders.

Perhaps Olsky wanted payback for a recent public embarrassment. In 1934, while performing his "important work in nutrition" (Stalin's words), Olsky fell victim to Valya Egorov, a 12-year-old canteen inspector kleptomaniac who stole a watch from Olsky's office. If

Egorov ever existed, it was not as he was portrayed. The story may have been a figment of Yagoda's imagination inspired by countless desperate orphans created by war and famine. The very real problem of orphan crime sparked a brutal legal change: by April 1935, twelve-year-olds became subject to trial, prison, hard labor, and execution.

Incidentally, Yagoda had already shown that the secret police were more than willing to work on the orphan problem. In Leningrad in 1933, Stalin complained about the young human "garbage" that was "littering the city". As a result, "about seven thousand street children were removed... to Siberia and other remote areas." [140]

Returning to our little watch-thief orphan Valya, his confession was publicized in the news. It made Olsky look inept. This little-known story was as blatantly false as the better-known tale of Pavel Morozov, the boy who denounced his own father as an enemy of the people, was murdered by his counter-revolutionary grandparents, and whose sacrifice was honored for decades with statues and stories (and his own postage stamp in 1950). It didn't matter that this story of brave little Pavlik was a lie. [3, 14, 8]

Olsky's insufficiently Bolshevik vigilance regarding his wristwatch didn't help. He was arrested in May 1937 and spent nearly half a year in prison. Number 91 on the 1 November 1937 kill list, he was shot on 27 November. [21]

An unnamed wife apparently was sent to the camps, an elder son into the abyss of state orphanages, and a younger son to stay with relatives. As for Olsky, he was cremated, his ashes dumped into Donskoye cemetery's Common Grave Number 1.

Sergei Vasilievich Puzitsky

1895 or 1898 - 1937

Mass deporter and slave camp commander

Russia's modern SVR gives Puzitsky a positive official biography: he worked in military tribunals and OGPU counterintelligence. [23]

After military school and a stint as an artillery commander, Puzitsky joined the Cheka as a tribunal investigator. By his early twenties he was seeking out counter-revolutionaries and spies. He also gained a degree from the law school at Moscow University. Many of his professors would later die in the 1930s purges.

In 1921-22, age 23 or so, he headed one of the Cheka's many "special" departments to pursue enemies of the state. He worked in Operations Trust and Syndicate-2. Perhaps for helping to throw Boris Savinkov out a window, Dzerzhinsky gave him the agency's top prize, a gold-plated gun, inscribed for his "merciless fight against counterrevolution". [23]

In 1928 he and stamp man Syroezhkin went to Yakutia to kill the "White Guard" group and its Japanese masters, and in 1930 he organized Demidenko's Paris kidnapping job. [72]

In 1930-31 Puzitsky and stamp man Olsky deported hundreds of thousands of Ukrainian and North Caucasus farmers. Over time the Soviet Union forced more than two million people into freight trains to start remote "special" settlements, cut trees, dig mines, or build farms. Many would die enroute way or in their new work.

Puzitsky's secret study of the initial 1930-31 mass exile showed it was a deadly, expensive mess. His report makes clear that the OGPU was expanding mass exiles, particularly to the North. [17, 146]

To learn what these deportations were like on the receiving end, we can read a typical OGPU status report from Arkhangelsk, which in four days (26 Feb-1 Mar 1930) received five trainloads of exiles from southern Russia and Ukraine totaling 8,501 people, ranging from infants to ordinary adults to amputees to people more than ninety years old. More than three thousand were children. The OGPU's receiving officials stated that 72.2% of the exiles were incapacitated, some completely. The report mentions only old age and amputation as causes, but we can surmise that thousands of these exiles were living skeletons from the raging famine in the south. About two thousand people who seemed somewhat able-bodied were sent immediately to logging and other hard labor. The temperature was well below freezing, so many of those people soon died in the snow. 6,500 exiles unable to work were simply put in storage (with unknown fates): 1,310 in a factory space, another 1,342 in warehouse space at the port, and 3,901 stuffed into an old movie theater and a church. The OGPU report also included rumors, including a reference to a decade earlier: "Kedrov and Plastinina have arrived in Arkhangelsk, so now they will begin to gather up and shoot." Mikhail and Rebekka's reputation had lived on. *[154]*

Returning to Puzitsky, his truthful assessment of mass exile problems was politically dangerous. This may explain his demotion to a 1935-37 deputy chief at Camp 3 of Dmitlag, an NKVD labor camp whose residents were building the 80-mile-long Moscow-Volga Canal. Puzitsky's office was in the town of Dmitrov, in the Boris and Gleb monastery. He ran the Third Department—independent of the head of the camp, he developed informants and looked for anti-Soviet sentiment, sabotage, banditry, and whatever else could be concocted.

Although a small quantity of excavation machinery arrived late in the canal project, two hundred thousand canal workers used shovels, pick-axes, and their bare hands. Tens of thousands died from hunger, cold, exhaustion, beating, drowning, or accident. Some got grave-markers; many were dumped in the canal earthworks. However, as with the recent 75-mile White Sea Canal, this new one was officially the result of "heroic work". *[5, 10, 12, 79]*

We do not know if Puzitsky began a detailed operational assessment of the labor camp and the construction of the Moscow-Volga canal. There is no canal version of his scathing 1930 mass exile assessment. He was arrested in 1937 with other canal bosses, just weeks before the canal's official opening. Perhaps an NKVD agent kept Puzitsky's gold-plated gun. On 29 May, NKVD chief Yezhov sent to Stalin a transcript of Puzitsky's interrogation (which was dated 29 April). Puzitsky confessed to joining a canal boss conspiracy in which up to 35,000 workers would march on Moscow to help seize power. (We presume all these traitors armed with digging tools were no longer exhausted by their heroic work on the canal). *[145]*

Puzitsky was number 24 on 16 June 1937's kill list. His ashes were dumped in Donskoye's Common Grave Number 1. *[11, 21, 72]*

His younger brother **Vladimir** was arrested in 1938 but lived. Vladimir's son wrote about his uncle and developed a family tree showing that Puzitsky's wife **Larisa Fedorovna Sereda** (a ballerina) and her mother went off to the camps. The mother died, but Larisa survived, died in the 1960s at age 66, and supposedly is buried in Moscow's Vostryakovsky cemetery. *[56, 72]*

Summer construction on the Moscow-Volga Canal

Women prisoners digging the Moscow-Volga Canal in winter

Drawings by a Dmitlag prisoner: A camp officer sprays a female prisoner with a hose while a soaked inmate shivers. [20]

Puzitsky's wife Larisa Fedorovna Sereda in costume

Vladimir Andreevich Styrne

1897 - 15 November 1937

Inquisitor of starving peasants

Styrne's evolution

1920s boy-ish   *1920s airbrushed*   *Stern Chekist*

Like Demidenko and Olsky, Russia's modern SVR ignores Styrne. He was born into a Latvian family. The official story is that his father died before Styrne was ten. By his late teens he and his mother were in Moscow. He became assistant chief of city census statistics. He joined the "active" side of Soviet power and helped repress a 1918 revolt in Moscow and enforce Soviet rule in 1920 in Kyrgyzstan.

He soon found a Chekist job assigned to none other than Joseph Stalin, the Commissar of Nationalities, who was forcing ethnic groups and countries into the new Soviet Union. Subjugating agricultural regions like Ukraine, Volga, Crimea, Samara, and Kazakhstan enabled the Soviets to export grain to buy the foreign equipment needed to build new heavy industry. Unfortunately, huge grain requisitions plus bad weather, shrinking acreage, war, and Soviet mismanagement, created a full-blown famine.

Styrne's task was to find spies in the 120,000 local workers of the American Relief Administration (ARA). Herbert Hoover created the ARA at the end of World War I to fight European starvation and disease. Gaining permission to distribute food in the Soviet Union took many attempts to get Lenin simply to admit the famine.

The US had donated food before in the 1891-92 Russian famine. The 1920-23 famine was worse. The ARA fed up to ten million Soviets a day, but several million still starved to death. In retrospect, Hoover has been credited with direct responsibility for saving more human lives than any other person in history.

The Cheka watched the ARA closely. In November 1921 in Samara, for example, where the terrible famine was worsening, the local Cheka chairman knew logistical details of the ARA's new work plan to feed children in the province. Numerous officials reported on ARA details like the number of feeding stations in a particular county or the number of meals provided to children. Many reports also made clear that Chekists and Soviet government officials too were in dire straits—hungry, but at least not starving to death. *[116, 117, 118]*

Part of the Cheka's famine work was to fight "banditry", which included things like violent insurrection, robbery, murder, and cannibalism, all driven by desperate hunger and the social breakdown exacerbated by the Soviet government's own policies.

The Cheka also combated what they termed capitalist "speculators"—people who left for other regions to attempt to "illegally" buy food and bring it to their starving families and towns.

While ARA fed the starving, Styrne and his Chekists interrogated ARA's Soviet workers people for signs of disloyalty—friendliness with foreigners, talking too freely, expressing admiration, complaining about Bolsheviks. Virtually any interaction or information-gathering about the famine could be anti-Soviet espionage. Even a dentist who helped the ARA was sentenced to Solovki. [166, p. 109-110]

One of their subjects, for example, was 29-year-old William Shafroth, the son of a former Colorado governor, a war veteran, and an ARA worker whom the Cheka identified as the leader of a group of American intelligence agents. Shafroth's urgent task was to organize a monumental relief effort. This required travel and field research and of course the American government was interested in such information. Still, this instance highlights the Cheka's incurable suspicion of foreigners, even in the face of obvious efforts to prevent millions of their fellow citizens from starving to death. [119, 120]

America finally ended the ARA free food program when the Cheka refused, in the midst of self-induced starvation, to stop seizing and exporting domestic crops. Soviet ships were being loaded with export grain while the ARA unloaded grain to feed starving people.

*80 famine victims, mostly children, piled in a graveyard, Samara 1921
(Nansen photos/Amer. Red Cross, Library of Congress)*

Styrne rose through the Cheka's ranks. He ran punitive departments, joined Operation Trust, and worked in the East, Russia, Moscow, Turkestan and other places. *[15]*

He also did field work for the Ukrainian NKVD for a number of years. On 10 July 1930, the Soviet Union's Politburo officially approved, among other things, a list from Styrne's local office to execute 276 people as kulaks, 66 as criminals, and to exile 1293 kulaks and 425 criminals. The total number of executions approved in this one Politburo document was about 25,000 people. *[152]*

In 1935 he reported on sabotage and arrests, and identified villagers who were morally decayed, drunk, embezzlers, etc. In 1936 he reported on agricultural failures and the punishment of saboteurs and malingerers, and noted that farm workers would not have sufficient food supplies. In 1937 he identified institutional failures and factory-peasant competition for food. *[147, 148, 149, 150]*

On 20 July 1937, Styrne became new chief of the Third Division (the counterintelligence office) of the Ukrainian NKVD, filling a vacancy caused by the sudden departure of David Moiseevich Sokolinsky, who held the post for only three months before being transferred. Sokolinsky ended up as number 276 on the 16 January 1940 kill list and was shot. *[21]*

Styrne was a good choice for his new management position—he knew Ukraine well, and his math background and census work stood out. His many field reports show he methodically gathered and analyzed data. Year after year, he provided data and factual commentary and carefully avoided opinion and personal judgment.

He clearly knew what was happening. Mikhail Shreider, a close colleague in the Ivanovo office Styre managed, wrote that Styrne was nervous to return to Moscow for meetings, and that he started leaving work early to avoid hearing prisoners being tortured in a nearby office. Styrne advised Shreider to obey orders and keep quiet. *[186]*

Styrne moved to Kyiv with his wife Alexandra Ivanovna who apparently also worked for the NKVD (we will learn more about her in a couple of pages). The couple (we don't know if they had any children) moved into Apartment 41 at 36 Karl Liebknecht Street, now Shovkovychna (Mulberry) Street, an elegant building overlooking tranquil parks. Perhaps Styrne ate on the balcony and read work papers, or thought about people he saw starve in the 1920s while he investigated the American Relief Agency. Presumably today's apartment residents do not know about the former occupants. *[185]*

Styrne's apartment building:
36-7 Shovkovychna Street, Kyiv (Source: Google Maps)

Even a dedicated Soviet would have suffered in Styrne's field work. Years of measuring famine, desperation, and corruption could not have left him unchanged.

We can look at a younger Styrne, and we can see his last known picture, which shows the face of a well-fed Chekist (or maybe one who drank a lot). Maybe it is just a typical employee identification photo. Maybe it shows the weary face of a witness to years of mass hunger and starvation. Maybe it is the doomed look of a man being arrested by his own agency.

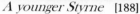

A younger Styrne [188]   *Late in his career*

Like many, Styrne "knew too much and was involved in such events, the truth of which was of a 'dangerous' nature, and was therefore doomed to go into oblivion". Many Ukraine NKVD officers were arrested in the mid-to-late 1930s. *[159, p. 569, 589-594]*

If destiny exists, then three factors suggest that Styrne was truly destined to be shot.

First, he could see that many longtime career Chekists like himself were being shot. His aforementioned colleague Mikhail Shreider from Ivanovo noted Styrne's growing nervousness. *[186]*

Second, Styrne was ethnically Latvian (even though he managed to have his papers identify him as Russian). The NKVD was busy with its Latvian Operation, in which thousands of ethnic Latvians (including various Styrnes, Styrns, and Styrnas) were shot.

Third, we must remember Styrne's first job. Recall that before his years of rural investigation he started with the seemingly safe and innocuous job of an assistant chief in Moscow's census department.

The first comprehensive Soviet Union population census took place in 1926. The next one, in early 1937, inconveniently revealed millions of rural and Gulag deaths. In an elegantly durable solution, Stalin suppressed the data and used the newspaper <u>Pravda</u> to blame enemies of the people for botching the project. Beginning in March 1937, census employees and statisticians across the country were shot.

So, if Styrne had stayed in the Moscow census office and not joined the Cheka, he probably would have been shot anyway.

Like his predecessor Sokolinsky, Styrne held his new Kyiv job for three months. Arrested with his wife in October 1937, he was sent to Moscow. He appeared on the 1 November kill list, but someone crossed out all the names. He reappeared on the 13 November list; two days later he was convicted and shot. *[21, 80]*

Styrne is in Donskoye's Common Grave Number 1. Later, he was official rehabilitated despite his years of destructive work. *[159, p. 13]*

His colleague Shreider remembered Styrne's wife as Alexandra Ivanovna, with a patronymic but an unknown maiden surname. No public records for Alexandra Ivanovna Styrne were located.

There is, however, an extremely brief 1938 death record for one Alexandra Andreevna *Ivanova*, said to have been born in 1901 in Voroshilov, the 1935 name for Nikolsk-Ussuriysk. She was shot on 10 March 1938 at the Butovo shooting ground outside Moscow, five months before Artur Artuzov's brother Rudolf was shot there. *[187]*

Several years younger than Styrne, this Ivanova was shot in Moscow several months after he was. Reading into the empty space of her death record, we can infer that she was someone distinctive. There is no more background, arrest or conviction information. This suggests data was censored, destroyed, or omitted. The various other Alexandria Ivanovas in such lists, and the vast majority of list members overall, have varied items like social class and/or work status, education, arrest reason, sentence, agency managing the case, and so on.

In contrast, this Alexandra Ivanova has a uniquely suitable blend of age, death date, death location, and obscured background to remain a possible candidate for Styrne's wife.

And, their patronymics are the same. Perhaps this Alexandra was indeed married to Vladimir Andreevich Styrne and Alexandra Ivanovna Styrne turned into Alexandra Andreevna Ivanova.

We can easily imagine a name change happening by accident, a drunken official transcribing the wrong information during a late night transfer and execution after having already dealt with so many thousands of shootings. We can also imagine it happening on purpose as a way for an official to conceal her death or spitefully erase her memory. We can even imagine the condemned prisoner hoping to buy time and suddenly inspired to give out an incorrect but similar name, hoping that the executioners might relent, thinking that the guards back at the prison had pulled out the wrong person. This is all speculation, and we may never know the truth, but something like this would explain Ivanova's remarkably blank death record.

We do not know what happened to Styrne's mother, or whether he had any siblings or children.

Grigori Sergeevich Syroezhkin

25 January 1900 - 1939
The human plague

Syroezhkin's stamp contains either a lie or a mistake. It says he died in 1937. Actually, he is number 111 on a 20 August 1938 kill list of former NKVD employees and was shot in early 1939. *[21, 25]*

The author of a 2009 Russian book about the Cheka, when seeking a chapter title for Syroezhkin, settled on what can be translated as "Man's Plague" or "The Plague of Humanity". *[25]*

That epithet seems to fit, but we must dig deep to ponder his real life. He was the most traveled, the most hands-on, and perhaps the most intriguing of the 2002 stamp men. The most personally brutal of the 2002 stamp men, he is in an odd way also the most tragic one.

Syroezhkin was born on 25 January 1900, to peasants in Volkovo, a tiny village in rural Balashov (Elan) district of Saratov province in southern Russia, which had been devastated by a horrific famine only eight years earlier. *[30]*

In 1905, the young family sought a better life and moved to Tbilisi, Georgia. His father found work in the local Russian Army garrison.

Syroezhkin's early life was a series of traumas and personal disappointments. Uprooted from his tiny Russian village at the age of five, he grew up as a poor foreigner in a big city under the yoke of the Russian Empire and in the turmoil of World War I. His father's low-level garrison job helped pay for an education as the way to a better life. Syroezhkin did well and passed multiple exams but seems to have been bullied by his better-off Tbilisi classmates. A physically energetic teenager, he tried to join the Russian Army at age 14 or 15 out of excitement or necessity but was sent home for being too young. He studied wrestling and tried to join a circus doing dramatic Cossack Dzhigitovka horse-riding stunts, but an injury ended that dream.

He found a stable job as a railway clerk but the Russian Revolution arrived and the Empire died. The Syroezhkins were now foreigners in Georgia. Somehow they made their way back to Volkovo, but life in southern Russia during the Civil War was extremely dangerous and profoundly difficult. Syroezhkin entered the Red Army (allegedly a volunteer, but very possibly a conscript), then moved into the Cheka. His Georgian schooling meant he was literate, a rarity among rural peasants and a big advantage. It seems he was a voracious reader.

Present-day Russia's SVR gives him a positive but innocuous biography. He served briefly as a Red Army soldier before becoming a tribunal commandant. By age 18 he had joined the Cheka, where he stood out as "completely satisfied...physically strong...impressed that the results of his operational work were immediate". [23]

Something in young Grisha's psychology led him to enjoy hurting people. His childhood seems to be the root of it all.

His 1924 file photo suggests a fighter and drinker, with a dark scar at the inside corner of his eye, baggy eyes, and maybe a broken nose. He appears much older than he is, and the photo is heavily edited. The unnatural sharp edges of very white areas suggest that details have been painted out.

Syroezhkin at age 23 or 24

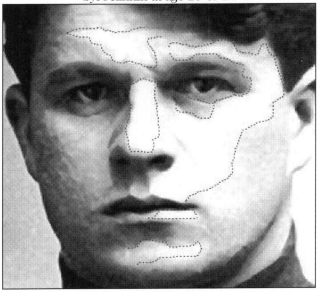

A 1937 photo hints at discolorations on the dark side of his face, and scars around his eye, on his lip and chin. These may be the elements edited out of his 1924 photo.

Syroezhkin, Spain, 1937 [32]

Moving from youth to adulthood, Syroezhkin continued his "operational" work, always as a busy hands-on enforcer. *[23, 25, 66]*

For two decades he traveled Asia and Europe, ranging as far east as China, Mongolia, and Kolyma, and as far west as Finland, Sweden, Germany, and Spain. Sometimes he traveled by choice, sometimes due to demotions for drinking. A severe alcoholic even by Soviet standards, by now he probably was not completely satisfied and guilt-free. His youthful injuries and the brutal nature of his "operational" Cheka work imply significant physical and emotional damage.

In Georgia and Chechnya in 1918-1920, he may have repressed bandits, anti-Soviets and kulaks. At age 20 or 21, back in Saratov oblast, Syroezhkin helped repress thousands in the "Popov gang". With hundreds of other "antibanditry" Chekists, he then helped repress the enormous Antonovshchina (Tambov Rebellion). Tens of thousands of peasants and army deserters fought against Bolshevik rule and grain confiscations. In return, the Red Army and Kedrov's Chekists used summary executions and poison gas. Up to 250,000 people may have died in the rebellion. *[13, 19]*

Bolsheviks release poison gas downwind against Tambov peasants, 1921

In Belarus in 1924 he eliminated the Ivanov and other gangs. Dzerzhinsky gave Syroezhkin a gold watch for this Belarus "work".

In Operation Trust he put a bullet in Sidney Reilly's chest. In Operation Syndicate-2 he interrogated Boris Savinkov and helped Puzitsky throw him out a Lubyanka window.

In Chechnya in 1925 he helped identify and eliminate bandits. In Yakutia in 1928 he eliminated a rebel group, then went to the Arctic and killed "spy" Yuri Schmidt, who was planning a major rebellion in the middle of nowhere with the help of wicked Americans—Syroezhkin got Schmidt drunk, took him outside, and killed him.

In 1928-29 he eliminated rebels and gangs in Buryatia, Kolyma and Mongolia. He crossed the border into China and killed anti-Soviet "nests" of hapless Russian refugees. In Novosibirsk he broke up the "Black" organization, arrested 300 peasants, and sentenced 73 to death. In Kamen-na-Obi and Chumakovsky, he was involved in torture, summary killings, and the burning of a village.

In Leningrad he lived in an exclusive central section of the city (Apt, 10, No. 8 Perovskaya St, now returned to its original name of Malaya Konyushennaya (Little Stable) Street), only a ten-minute walk from the Cheka's offices on Gorokhovaya, the base from which he "crushed" more than 136 Leningrad espionage and terrorist groups supposedly connected to General Kutepov, an anti-Soviet expatriate in Paris. Perhaps this means he hurt 136 people. *[185]*

To learn the identities of Kutepov's local plotters, it is claimed that handsome Syroezhkin used his Chekist charm to seduce an anti-Soviet former noblewoman so she would surrender the names of her allies. Considering that Syroezhkin was a violent young man of low education with an inferiority complex who spoke Russian with a rural or Georgian accent, seduction seems unlikely. We can conclude that he simply beat and/or raped a woman to extort information. *[31]*

He returned to Belarus to uncover, uproot, and liquidate enemies. In the 1932 Union of the Liberation of Belarus case, he helped jail or kill more than a hundred dangerous conspirators who had disguised themselves for decades as leading teachers, scientists, and writers.

In the mid-1930s, Syroezhkin traveled to Spain, where he "repeatedly personally participated in the implementation of special tasks" in the Spanish Civil War. One of his subordinates there was a translator from Paris, Lev Borisovich Savinkov (1912-1987), the son of Boris Savinkov, the man Syroezhkin threw out a window. Young Lev probably never knew his boss killed his father. Lev clearly bought into the party line—after World War II he helped rounded up Russians in France to be sent back to the camps. [29, 55]

A group photo in Spain is interesting. Among other things, these men helped evacuate (steal) 500 tons of Spanish gold to the Soviet Union for "safekeeping". Vasilevsky later was involved in the murder of Leon Trotsky in Mexico. Rabtsevich was from Belarus—he helped enforce Soviet power there by deportations and other methods until his retirement in 1952. Orlovsky was Belarusian as well—he killed farmers and had been an NKVD overseer of the Moscow-Volga Canal alongside stamp man Puzitsky.

Soviet spies, Madrid, August 1937. Front: L.P. Vasilevsky.
Rear left to right: A.M. Rabtsevich, G.S. Syroezhkin, K.P. Orlovsky. [32]

There is no known record of Syroezhkin having a wife or children. We do not know if his father Sergei Lavrentyevich Syroezhkin, mother Agafya Kirillovna, or younger brother Konstantin Sergeevich Syroezhkin survived the Civil War and the subsequent famines and ravages of the young Soviet Union.

Syroezhkin's time in the Madrid NKVD residency was his last significant assignment. He committed the sin of honesty—he told friends that he believed in the innocence of certain senior Red Army officers who had been shot. Someone betrayed his confidence. He was number 111 on the kill list for 20 August 1938, but being in Spain gave him a little extra time. *[21]*

In late 1938, Moscow ordered him to return. Syroezhkin knew by then that many of his colleagues had been killed and that people were being shot or sent to the camps in prodigious numbers. The Soviet Union had always been a dangerous place for its citizens, but this current frenzy of bloodletting had lasted more than two years.

Syroezhkin was more than a thousand miles from the USSR. He was an experienced international traveler who could avoid Soviet foreign agents. There is no evidence of a wife or children to protect. He knew well that the Soviet Union was brutal and dysfunctional.

He was the only stamp man who had some real freedom to determine his fate once the walls began to close in. He certainly knew what was happening, and he was well-positioned to escape. He had a very real chance to survive. Still, he chose to follow orders rather than disappear or defect.

Did he fear for his parents, brother, unknown loved ones, or Chekist friends in Moscow? Did he fear for hometown relatives and their friends? Numerous Syroezhkins and others from his hometown were being deported to Kazakhstan and Tomsk region. *[234]*

Was he after all these terrible years a dedicated loyalist blind to his likely fate? He knew that many of his colleagues with greater rank, education, and influence were dead. He had known the other stamp men for two decades and watched as they rose to high levels in the Cheka, but he was doing the same rough work he began twenty years earlier. By his late thirties, he must have understood that a cynical bureaucracy viewed him merely as a tool to be used. His life experience and habitual drinking suggest he was deeply unhappy..

Syroezhkin's return to Moscow seems foolish, but perhaps was driven by family concerns. One source says he registered at the Hotel Moscow, where some unnamed-but-not-yet-dead friend supposedly phoned him about a new decree to recognize the work of outstanding intelligence officers in Spain. Syroezhkin certainly would have seen this for the lie it was. Perhaps he wore his Belarus gold watch when he went downstairs, bought a bottle of liquor to share with his friend, and found three agents who held out his arrest warrant. [29]

During the infamously cold winter of 1938-39 he was convicted as a Polish spy. According to NKVD records, he lost his job on 21 January 1939 and was arrested 8 February. On 26 February 1939, barely 39 years old, he was convicted and shot. [29, 30, 64]

He was the last of the 2002 stamp men. It must have been a strange feeling, knowing that his colleagues were gone. Never again would they meet for lunch or enjoy drinks after a long day. Never more could they share travel stories or throw someone out a window.

It should come as no surprise that Syroezhkin was cremated and joined his colleagues in Donskoye's Common Grave Number 1.

Think back to Syroezhkin as a child. That strong little boy, with some luck or kindness, could have become someone completely different. Instead, shaped by poverty, war, and Russia's new Bolshevik overlords, he hurt and destroyed people for two decades.

6. 1937: Washed away

Let Russia serve as a lesson...
the mountains of corpses...the oceans of blood...
Maximoff, The Guillotine at Work, 1940

THEY WADED INTO BLOOD as young men. Five of the 2002 stamp men were washed away before turning forty. Their agency killed at least five of them.

All six outlived their mentor Felix Dzerzhinsky. He died in 1926, officially by heart attack, most likely by poison. With flawless timing, Iron Felix received his own stamps in 1936, as his old agency was preparing its enormous surge. Lest the public forget his all-seeing eye, he received more stamps in 1951, 1962, and 1977. *[22, 34]*

In the early 1930s, the Soviet Union demanded canals for its radiant future. Gulag prisoners clawed the White Sea and Moscow-Volga canals into existence, and more were in the works. Never mind that the canals were too shallow for most ships—the Cheka soon received new orders. The stamp men and their colleagues clambered atop the agency's floodgates, flexed their muscles, and cranked the gates open for a new torrent of blood on a unfathomable scale.

The red tsunami had many names: the Great Purge, the Great Terror, and the Yezhovshchina (after five-foot-tall Nikolai Yezhov, the NKVD's energetic chief). Most simply, the flood was called 1937.

Excluding deaths in interrogation, transit, exile and the camps, from 1936 to 1938 the NKVD carefully documented the direct execution of nearly 700,000 people.

7. Washed away, but not forgotten

The memory of dead Chekists lives on...

Pioneer Truth, 21 December 1932

ALTHOUGH THE LAST of the 2002 stamp men was shot more than eighty years ago, they survive to varying degrees in the collective consciousness due to past and present reinforcement. Some are mostly forgotten, others remembered as heroes.

<u>Individual stamp men</u>

Artur Artuzov is the best known. A memorial stone at Donskoye cemetery's Common Grave Number 1 is encircled by small plaques naming a few of the thousands of people whose ashes were dumped in the pit between 1930 and 1942. By 2018, someone (probably Putin's government) added a rather large granite plaque for Artuzov.

Elsewhere, a 2017 bust and board in his home district identify him as a "Genius of Intelligence" and celebrate the centennial of Russian security forces. The bust faces Kashin's central square from the front of Proletariat Street No. 15, home of Kashinskaya Gazeta, the official local newspaper since 1918. Artuzov's ninety-year-old niece, a nephew, and other relatives gathered for the unveiling of their ancestor's head in the decaying city. In news photos, they seemed quite unaware of the irony of honoring a killer of independent thought in front of a state-approved newspaper. *[38]*

Artuzov also has new memorial plaques in his home village of Ustinovo, in #9 Milutinsky Lane in Moscow where he lived, and at St. Petersburg's Polytechnic University where he went to college.

Earlier, in 2001, Artuzov's old friend and assistant Boris Gudz—ancient but still breathing—was named the first recipient of Russia's new Artuzov award to honor service in counterintelligence. Presumably he received the award to inspire positive memories of Artuzov and counterintelligence in interviews, and not for his years as a Moscow bus-driver, or for ruining and outliving his three sisters.

Despite decades of change requests, the name of Artuzov's uncle Kedrov still adorns a street in Arkhangelsk, as does Dzerzhinsky's.

Demidenko gained no great recognition beyond a 1981 movie role. Olsky has his brief biography on Belarus's KGB website. Puzitsky stars in 1968 and 1981 films about Operation Syndicate-2, and has a brief positive biography from the SVR. Styrne is in a mid-1960s move about Operation Trust. More recently, he was identified as the recipient of secret internal memoranda about the truth of the shooting and burial of British agent Sidney Reilly. *[2, 23, 53]*

Syroezhkin may be the most remarkable of all, emerging from his communal grave not only as a cinematic working-class Chekist hero with a positive SVR biography, but with his own boat.

The *Grigory Syroezhkin* , a 43-foot (13.3 meter) KS-110 class boat with shipyard construction number 178 was commissioned by the Russian government on May 25, 2007. Suitably, the boat was given to the Cheka's descendant, the FSB, and assigned to a Yakutsk-based fleet on the Lena River. Syroezhkin knew this area well—he spent several years killing his way through Siberia and the Russian Far East. Records suggest the boat is an unremarkable border guard patrol boat. No pictures were found, and information is scarce. *[27, 28]*

Syroezhkin's boat reminds us of an earlier ship, the 1990s border patrol frigate *Kedrov*, named for Artuzov's uncle Mikhail, whose Arkhangelsk camps inspired the Gulag.

Border patrol ship "Kedrov", from navsource.narod.ru

Interestingly, the village of Kholmogory, known mostly for carved bones and a Kedrov-Artuzov concentration camp, has *two* ships named for it. The small Baltic freighter *Kholmogory* (built 1995) is based in Arkhangelsk. A 1998 fishing vessel of the same name is from Murmansk. Other boats and ships have been named for *Pertominsk* and other Gulag sites.

Although he moved to Georgia as a child, Syroezhkin has supporters in his birth-region. One Tatyana Sevostyanova (born Syroezhkina and apparently a family descendant), states "Syroezhkin G.S. Born and raised in my homeland. A memorial plaque is installed on the house." Another nearby supporter, one Anatoly Khoreshevsky, says Syroezhkin was "an outstanding man and an intelligence officer from the village behind our village." *[3]*

Syroezhkin's official re-vivification continues with a 2018 biography in the form of a radio documentary podcast "Gregory Syroezhkin: Camouflage-Man" by state-owned RIA Novosti (ria.ru) on its series Theory of Errors. *[4]*

Film and literary exploits

During Yuri Andropov's long tenure as KGB head, Soviet docu-drama cinema put carefully curated tales in popular imagination.

Operation Trust (Операция Трест) was a 5-hour 1967-8 mini-series about luring Sidney Reilly to Moscow. The operation was so familiar that Artuzov and Styrne were introduced by last name only. The real ending, in which Syroezhkin shot Reilly, was not included.

Crash (Крах), sometimes translated as Collapse, was a 3-hour 1968 movie about luring expatriate Boris Savinkov back to Moscow. It was the film version of the novel Retribution (Ardamatsky, 1967). The film and book were made together and could not emerge without the editorial approval and practical support of the KGB. The cast included Dzerzhinsky, Artuzov, Puzitsky, and Syroezhkin.

Syndicate-2 (Синдикат-2), a 1981 remake of Crash as a 6-part television mini-series, adds stamp man Demidenko as Savinkov's confessor. Neither Crash nor Syndicate-2 showed Savinkov's real-life bone-crushing demise in a Lubyanka courtyard.

Heroic literature about Operations Trust and Syndicate-2 shows the all-seeing and scrupulously clean Cheka/OGPU, tireless Dzerzhinsky, brilliant Artuzov, and shrewd but doomed enemies.

Two versions from one author show how truth evolves. In Gladkov's 1983 version, British spy O'Reilly (Operation Trust) is executed without details, traitor Savinkov (Syndicate-2) is sentenced to death but set free, and Artuzov simply ends with no explanation. Gladkov's 2008 version admits the late-night shooting of O'Reilly, Savinkov's execution, and Artuzov's death due to bureaucratic feuding. Both books include quotes from Artuzov's sisters, suggesting they survived the executions of two brothers and sister-in-law Inna. In an aside, Gladkov translates as "Smooth". *[53, 54]*

Operation Trust

Artuzov

Styrne

Crash

Dzerzhinsky

Artuzov

Puzitsky

Syroezhkin

Syndicate-2

Dzerzhinsky

Artuzov

Demidenko

Puzitsky

Syroezhkin

8. The Cheka's century

[T]he unsheathed sword....must always be ready.

Pioneer Truth, 21 December 1932

FOR MORE THAN a century, the secret police has exerted its influence and hewed to its essential nature. We see this in the history of the agency's leadership and the country's leadership.

<u>Leaders of the secret police</u>

Felix Edmundovich Dzerzhinsky, the founding face of the Cheka, died in 1926 after a long, highly critical speech about the dense Soviet bureaucracy. It seems he was poisoned on Stalin's orders.

Yakov Khristoforovich Peters briefly served as interim chairman for five weeks in 1918. In 1938 he was arrested and shot.

Vyacheslav Rudolfovich Menzhinsky, Dzerzhinsky's deputy since 1919, took over when his boss died. Menzhinsky developed apparent heart trouble in the late 1920s but continued to work as a semi-invalid. He expired on 10 May 1934, ostensibly by illness but likely aided by poison from his deputy, who had been doing Menzhinsky's work for years and was about to lead the creation of a new agency.

Genrikh Grigoryevich Yagoda, Menzhinsky's deputy, took over when his boss died. He later confessed to killing Menzhinsky, which may be true—one of Yagoda's tasks was running a poison laboratory for the secret police. As new NKVD chief, Yagoda cleaned shop. He oversaw Artuzov's continuing demotions and may have killed Demidenko. He demoted Olsky and humiliated him with the Egorov watch thief story. He expanded Puzitsky's deportations and demoted Puzitsky to camp management. The last two stamp men, Styrne and Syroezhkin, avoided Yagoda's direct ire but would meet their fate soon enough. Yagoda lasted a little more than two years as chief. He was demoted in 1936, arrested in 1937, tried in 1938, and shot.

Nikolai Ivanovich Yezhov replaced his mentor Yagoda then arranged his arrest, torture, trial, and execution. He oversaw the Great Purge which washed away Styrne and Syroezhkin. Yezhov's zealous over-fulfillment of purge quotas was not rewarded—he was removed in late 1938, tortured, and put on secret trial. In early 1940, in an execution basement he himself had designed, Yezhov was shot.

Lavrentiy Pavlovich Beria engineered Yezhov's demise and took his job. Beria was born less than two hundred miles from his fellow Georgian Joseph Stalin. By 1922 he had overcome Mikhail Kedrov's intrigues in Baku and was running Georgia's OGPU as Stalin's trusted fist. After replacing Yezhov, he ran internal affairs for fifteen years, effectively institutionalizing the Gulag system. When Stalin died in 1953, Beria at first appeared to be winning a top-level struggle to run the country, but he was out-maneuvered, arrested, tried, and shot.

From 1953 to 1967, and from 1982 to the end of 1991, there were various secret police chiefs. Some lasted a year or two, some five or six. In between those shorter-termed chiefs was Yuri Andropov.

Yuri Vladimirovich Andropov ran the KGB for fifteen years (1967-82). A 1930s Cheka informer, he became the driving force in the 1956 Soviet invasion of Hungary. As Soviet leader Leonid Brezhnev's longtime secret police chief, Andropov used prison and deportation to stifle almost all political dissent. He finally got to run the entire country, but lasted only fifteen months before dying.

Vladimir Aleksandrovich Kryuchkov, the next to last head of the KGB, attempted a coup in mid-1991 to force General Secretary Gorbachev to clamp down on dissent and restore order in the rapidly disintegrating Soviet Union. The plot, which intended to rely on the power of the police state to restore order, failed. Kryuchkov was briefly imprisoned, then amnestied to live free for years.

Vadim Viktorovich Bakatin, the last secret police chief before the Soviet Union collapsed, spent late 1991 trying to take apart the organization, intending to change the culture and close the bureaucratic section which stifled domestic dissent. Bakatin believed that it was self-destructive to monitor, muzzle, and punish citizens for independent thought. Ironically, he used language typical of a Chekist to express his view: "The traditions of chekism must be eradicated, must cease to exist as an ideology." *[35]*

Partly because he relied on change from within, rather than a dramatic old-style house-cleaning purge, Bakatin failed. The gears of Lenin's Cheka machine would grind on, outliving the Soviet government it had so long dominated.

Chekists and the leaders of the Soviet Union/Russia

Looking from Stalin's time to the end of the Soviet Union, the police state became more entwined with national (party) leadership and, at the same time, became more incapable. Now, in a remarkable reversal, since the demise of the Soviet Union the police state has become even more entwined, and increasingly capable.

Lavrenty Beria, whom Stalin introduced as "our Himmler" to Franklin Roosevelt and Winston Churchill at the 1945 Yalta conference, came close to mastering the Soviet Union after Stalin's death, but only for a few weeks. A notorious rapist and torturer, Beria was arrested for treason, tried, convicted, and shot.

Nikita Sergeyevich Khrushchev, Beria's successor, worked with, made use of, and was beholden to the secret police. As a Communist Party official, he was involved for decades with the Cheka, but not truly part of them. Khrushchev use their labor to build the Moscow subway system in the early 1930s, then signed off on orders to arrest or execute of tens of thousands of Muscovites. In Ukraine in early 1938 he oversaw bloody repressions and deportations. He arrived a couple of months after stamp man Styrne was killed, and moved into a mansion at Shovkovychna 14, a short walk up the street from Styrne's old apartment. Khrushchev eventually lost his job in part because his reformist "anti-fear" policies threatened the Cheka's bureaucratic status quo. He retired in 1964, but was not shot.

Leonid Ilyich Brezhnev, a Party official whom Khrushchev had mentored for years, repaid the favor by engineering his patron's removal and taking his job. The long "Brezhnev stagnation" was characterized by bureaucratic and economic sclerosis; complainers were muzzled by Andropov's KGB. As a youth, Brezhnev was a Party propagandist, whatever that means. He worked alongside the OGPU to forcibly collectivize agriculture in a most interesting place-- near the family farm of a later Russian leader, Boris Yeltsin. *[36]*

Brezhnev clung to his job for 18 years and died in office a decrepit old man in 1982.

Yuri Vladimirovich Andropov, the now equally decrepit Chekist who squelched dissenters during Brezhnev's reign, moved into his boss's job, refused to retire, and died just over a year later in 1984.

Konstantin Ustinovich Chernenko, an even more decrepit apparatchik, succeeded Andropov. Chernenko was a career propagandist who had been an OGPU border guard on the Kazakhstan-Chinese frontier from 1930-1933. We don't know what he did there—maybe nothing significant, or maybe some of the same ruthless killing that stamp man Syroezhkin did in the region. Public biographical information on Chernenko's time as an OGPU guard is very sparse—perhaps his background was impressive, embarrassing, dull, or awful. Whatever the youthful truth, Chernenko was in truth terminally ill when he took the Soviet Union's leadership post, General Secretary of the Communist Party. He died almost exactly eleven months later, in 1985.

From a managerial or institutional point of view, the best way to grasp this appointment of the remarkably useless Chernenko to understand it as the culmination of decades of profound bureaucratic blight created by the Cheka.

Mikhail Sergeyevich Gorbachev, the intelligent, energetic and youthful last leader of the Soviet Union, was a career Communist Party official but not a Chekist. As the first and last Soviet leader since Khrushchev to openly push for systemic change, Gorbachev was a controversial figure. His basic attitudes went against long-standing norms. Many people openly criticized him, many others openly admired him. Quite unlike his predecessors, he had what one Soviet Politburo member called a "spirit of...self-critical optimism". *[40]*

He ran the country from 1985 until Christmas Day 1991. The next day the legislature voted itself and the Soviet Union out of existence.

Boris Nikolayevich Yeltsin, the first president of post-Soviet Russia, was not a Chekist but knew their impact intimately.

In 1930, months before Yeltsin's birth, the government seized his grandfather's family farm. Perhaps during that time the grandfather met young Leonid Brezhnev, who was beginning his career of dedicated service to the masses by forcing farmers in Yeltsin's area to give up their fields and become laborers for the state. Perhaps Yeltsin, still in his mother's womb, passed near the future Soviet leader who was helping to ruin the family's life. There would be justice, of sorts, but it would take more than seventy years before Boris Yeltsin would walk past Brezhnev's official portraits as he walked down the halls of government.

We do not know if Yeltsin ever knew about young Brezhnev. Eventually Yeltsin's grandfather was sent off to die, exiled outside the steel mill town of Nadezhdinsk (now Serov), several hundred miles south of the Arctic Circle. In 1934, when Yeltsin was three, his father Nikolai was arrested and spent three years in Dmitlag, the Moscow-Volga slave labor camp which stamp man Puzitsky helped run.

We can be certain that Gulag prisoner Nikolai Yeltsin did not think that his fearsome camp officer Sergei Puzitsky would be on a postage stamp seven decades later.   Unlike Puzitsky, Nikolai Yeltsin survived the experience.   *[36]*

We can be equally certain that prisoner Yeltsin never suspected that his own son Boris would become president of Russia, or that his son would hand-pick a Chekist to succeed him.

And, we can be utterly certain that Gulag prisoner Yeltsin never imagined that his son would help renew the power of the secret police by making Chekist's Day an official annual holiday in 1995.

And now we come to the man who authorized commemoration of the stamp men.

Vladimir Vladimirovich Putin, a modern career Chekist, was mentored and lifted up by none other than Boris Yeltsin, a man whose parents and grandparents were traumatized by the Cheka.

Putin, a sixteen-year counterintelligence KGB agent, joined Saint Petersburg Mayor Yeltsin's office and became rich there. When the Soviet Union collapsed, Boris Yeltsin became president and made Putin his prime minister. We do not know if Putin got the job because of merit or if his promotion was due to other reasons.

Putin is the first career Chekist to reach the top and stay there. For two decades he has been the Russian government's effective head, rotating for constitutional reasons between prime minister and president. His rotational partner, Dmitri Anatolyevich Medvedev, has long-standing ties to the KGB's Putin, perhaps as early as college.

After the tumult of the 1990s, Putin has revitalized Russia's secret police with some modernizing, re-organizing and re-naming.

Suspicion and self-deception: Old Chekist

In its present form, the century-old Cheka has many well-trained and professional, serious and dedicated members. Nonetheless, ancient impulses still guide state security's limbic system. We can expect that the powerful influence, historical perception, and ingrained culture of the Cheka will continue.

Intelligence-gathering is important. We look for external threats and opportunities, and monitor internal strengths, weaknesses, and potential problems. We look before we cross the street, and go to the doctor for periodic check-ups. Families watch neighborhoods and children's behavior. Companies study their industries and use internal control processes and audits. Governments keep an eye on potential adversaries and have police to look for those who would do harm from within. These things are necessary and normal.

However, if a protective function is colored by strong suspicion and fear, and is coupled with self-deception and a propensity for violent reaction against threats real or imagined, then we, or our families, or our companies, or our countries, suffer. Those traits make discussion, negotiation, and change difficult. They encourage self-destructive reactions to threats real or imagined. And as we have seen they are, in the long run, not particularly helpful. Destructive suspicion and self-deception are common in many places, but they are deeply rooted in the Chekist mindset.

Let us move back in time to the third Wednesday of December 1932 and pick up a copy of Pioneer Truth, the newspaper for adolescents and young teens. It is a special occasion, the official commemoration of the fifteenth anniversary of Soviet intelligence, but the tone is routinely Bolshevik: uncompromising, reducing people to political elements, and inciting to violence. *[16]*

Pioneer Truth, No. 124, 21 December 1932

Chekist Number 1, Felix Dzerzhinsky, stares into the distance.

The lead article celebrates the Cheka-OGPU's fifteen year history of "proletarian struggle...Red Terror...[and] huge educational work to convert former enemies into workers". The secret police promise (threaten?) to "remain the unsheathed sword of the working class, neatly and skillfully driving away the enemy..."

Comrade Stalin offers greetings to the unsheathed sword, which is now becoming his personal blade. He will wield it frequently.

Mikhail Kalinin, chairman of the Soviet Union's Central Executive Committee, praises Chekist guardianship. He does not know that in a few years they will arrest his wife Ekaterina, torture her, and ship her off to camp until 1945. He will meekly continue in his government figurehead job.

Kalinin's co-signer, Avel Yenukidze, secretary of the same committee, is the godfather of Stalin's second wife Nadezhda. He must at this moment be very upset. His dear young Nadezhda has just killed herself, traumatized by her husband, several weeks before this newspaper. No matter. Yenukidze himself will be shot in 1937.

A dramatic story reports the murder of Kolya Myagatin, a good Soviet collective farm-boy who reported bread thieves. The paper promises no mercy for the captured counterrevolutionaries (presumably they were hungry). They will be dealt with in court. The paper urges schoolchildren to protect workers and collective farmers from the brutal attack of the class enemy.

Last but not least, "Old Chekist" offers up a free-form message (perhaps some would call it a poem) to Soviet children. The young author, Semyen Kirsanov, will become a mainstay of Soviet poetry and write a variety of propagandistic newspaper poems. Already in 1932, we can see his method (groveling imagery and glorified paranoia and violence, in the translation below.

"Старыи Чекист"

"Old Chekist", by Semyen Kirsanov
Cover of <u>Pioneer Truth</u>, No. 124, 21 December 1932

Translated by M. Pruett
following original format, punctuation, and verb tense shifts

NOTES:

"Star above a midnight visor" is a black-browed OGPU cap

"Central School" is the OGPU's cadet program

"Fourth year" refers to Year 4 of the USSR's first Five Year Plan

You know, friend,
   gray is no trifle.
How long have you
   been on vacation?
Work,
   work,
      work!–
Let it be so,
the same wrinkles cling to the temple...
You can
   (I know),
      old Chekist,
see
   the enemy's revolver,
so squeeze the enemy
   like a criminal brush,
to drop
  the gun
    to the feet.
But you know, friend,
   the heart's capacity for mercy,
and you shut off that valve.
By necessity,
   so that someone can await
the enemy
   with claws that catch.
The Chekist
   presses
     the call button,
Puts on his overcoat.
    He does not slouch.
Star
  above a midnight
    visor.
Together we go
  out to the street.
On Dzerzhinsky Street
a cadet
   passes by,
December in the window,
  knives sheathed,

footsteps crunch.
The wind has become
whirling snowfields,
  and slippery
    is the step.
And our eyes met a cadet
of the Central School.
He was much younger than us,
  wide-eyed,
eyebrows formed of
determination
   and excitement.
He comes,
   and the snow springs forth
a growing
   Chekist.
Reliable
   and Dzerzhinsky-like
students.
The fourth year
  of construction
is already
  buzzing,
and again the enemy
   begins to swarm
at our frontiers.
Day
  and night
we are on guard
  at pipelines
    and mines.
Still more
elders
Unsleepingly watch.
Yet all the scum is
  not finished off,
there is a crawling
  spider.
He will not pass
  and the span is complete —
the OGPU.

9. 2016-17: New gardener, new elephant

"Is it hard for you here?"
"It's hard everywhere", she answered cautiously...

M. Gorky, "Solovki" [179]

VLADIMIR PUTIN took office yet again as Russian president in 2016, replacing his placeholder Dmitri Medvedev.

On Christmas Eve 2016, Arkhangelsk installed a bust of Stalin, the Man of Steel and Gardener of Human Happiness, not in a public space but in a private car park behind the BUM shopping center, two blocks from Dzherzhinsky Prospect and a quarter-mile from the city's monument to victims of political repression. *[89, 90]*

As Arkhangelsk's new gardener mounted his modest pedestal, the city's waterfront witnessed the rebirth of Solzhenitsyn's mother tumor (see page 35) on Red Pier. Recall the Solovki camp acronym SLON (elephant). After trampling the city nearly a century ago, Slon was resurrected in late 2016-early 2017 as a 26-foot-high (8 meter) elephant made of discarded plastic bottles to promote a new restaurant with the same name. Internal lights illuminated it during the long winter nights.

Moscow's new gardener was not amused. Inspectors closed Slon Restaurant, the plastic bottle elephant sculpture was removed before the upcoming Arctic Forum biennial international conference, and Moscow decreed that the next Forum would move to St. Petersburg. *[84, 85, 86, 87, 88]*

10. 1992-2019: New flood, new stamp men

It is not heroes that make history, but history that makes heroes.

J.V. Stalin, Short Course, Ch. 1

SCIENTISTS IMPRISONED in laboratories. Murdered relatives. Deadly camps and prison construction projects. Young men who fought and died to preserve a system of fear.

First, we will note the many stamps from 1992-2019 related to the secret police. Second, we will take a close look at six new stamp men who appeared on 19 December 2018, one hundred years to the day after the Cheka created its counterintelligence Special Department.

A postal tsunami

This book's Appendix shows that post-Soviet Russia has issued more than 160 postage stamps with Chekist links, dozens in the last couple of years alone. Most are not directly about the secret police but have easily-uncovered connections to the agency's various incarnations from the Cheka to the present day. Stamps memorialize people, places, and events important in Soviet and Russian history. The fact that so many stamps have Chekist facets shows the pervasive and enduring influence of the police state, and the extensive yet often hidden or forgotten role of Chekists in history. Just beneath the surface of the present, the past still lies.

The new stamp men

Kravtsov   Kedrov   Zhidkov

Chebotarev   Abakumov   Krygin

The new stamp men

On 19 December 2018 (Chekists Day in Russia), the generally unknown Lugansk (Luhansk, in Ukrainian) People's Republic issued a rather limited edition (300) sheet of stamps to commemorate a century of military counterintelligence agencies. The LPR is a Russian-controlled proto-state which declared a disputed independence from Ukraine in 2014. The sheet features six new Soviet stamp men. It is from the LPR in name only. Russia provided the content, complex design, and high-quality production. *[83]*

The two center characters are Mikhail Kedrov, whom we already met, and Viktor Abakumov, who ran SMERSH (*Smert shpionem*—"death to spies"), the World War II counterintelligence agency designed to engage in counterintelligence and to watch the Red Army.

In 21st century Russia, SMERSH enjoys renewed celebration (without many details) for brilliance against the German enemy.

SMERSH was designed to work with the NKVD and also bypass it to provide Stalin with a bureaucratic counterweight. Abakumov rose through Beria's patronage but now he would report to Stalin.

SMERSH's purpose was inherently Chekist. SMERSH was intended to infiltrate its own country's military—the Red Army—to ensure loyalty to the Kremlin overlords.

These were the same Kremlin overlords who lobotomized the Red Army in the 1930s by killing tens of thousands of officers.

The same Kremlin overlords who aimed guns at the backs of Red Army soldiers to force them forward (Stalin's infamous Order 227, best known for its blunt "Not one step back").

The same Kremlin overlords who refused to sign the Geneva War Convention, who would not seek help for Soviet soldiers languishing in German prisoner-of-war camps, and who shipped tens of thousands of war prisoners (Germans, Poles, Japanese, and even a few Americans) off to Gulag labor camps.

The same Kremlin overlords who at the end of the war used the secret police to send trainloads of hundreds of thousands of returning Soviet soldiers off to Gulag camps (sometimes with the complicity of the West) for the crime of having been captured instead of killed or for having seen, by comparison with the West, how miserably the Soviet Union had failed its own citizens for nearly three decades.

The four peripheral figures on the stamp sheet were trained by SMERSH and worked and died as operational counterintelligence security officers in Red Army units during the Great Patriotic War. They are Grigory Kravtsov (age 22), Peter Zhidkov (age 43), Vasily Chebotarev (age 26), and Mikhail Krygin (age 27).

A SMERSH agent's job was to inspire his unit to fight against the Germans, to help the Red Army seek out German saboteurs, spies and sympathizers (of which there certainly were many), to work behind enemy lines at times, and to unmask Army malcontents, shirkers, and deserters. The Germans were profoundly brutal foreign invaders, but the Soviets themselves had already inflicted millions of deaths upon their own citizens. Millions more were being poured into the Soviet war grinder, and not all were enthused about the war effort or their country's leadership.

None of these stamp men had historically significant links to Ukraine or Luhansk which would be obvious reasons for issuing the stamps. Kravtsov was ethnically Ukrainian, but was born in Kazakhstan (probably to Ukrainians forced into exile) and died in Poland. Zhidkov, a Russian, died near Kyiv, but so did many others.

As noted, the LPR stamps were issued on 19 December 2018. Two days earlier, on 17 December, Russia issued sheets with different, romanticized portraits of the two youngest, Chebotarev and Krygin, just over one hundred years since their mid-1918 births. Chebotarev already had a museum exhibit in Belarus, and Krygin had a recent monument in Vladivostok.

So, why did Russia issue its new stamps in Lugansk?

Issuing the set in Russia could have been controversial—the two central figures Kedrov and Abakumov are well-known, admired by some, reviled by many.

Issuing them as LPR stamps was politically useful. The event was noted in various news outlets, reinforcing Moscow's message that the region is not Ukraine's Luhansk but the nominally independent state of Lugansk under Russian control. And, the stamps remind anyone paying attention of the nature of Soviet-style counterintelligence and secret police.

The LPR stamps are quintessentially Chekist. They strengthen political power by creating fear.

Grigory Mikhailovich Kravtsov

Grigory Mikhailovich Kravtsov (1922-45) was a Kazakh counter-intelligence officer. His stamp is a lie—he died not as a pilot but in an army punishment company composed of prisoners, one of thousands of such units in the most dangerous battlefield positions.

He is said to have been born on 15 March 1922 in the tiny Kazakhstan hamlet of Starozhilovka (now Kravtsovo in his honor), in the middle of nowhere on the railroad line between Chelyabinsk, Russia and Kostonay (Kustanai), Kazakhstan. His parents were Ukrainian: Mikhail Grigoryevich Kravtsov and Ustinya Borisovna Kravtsova. *[94, 111, 112]*

Why, one might ask, was a Ukrainian born in Kazakhstan? Two large Ukrainian groups came to northern Kazakhstan. First, settlers in the early 20th century before World War I used the railroad to move to sparsely-populated Kazakhstan in hopes of a better farm life. Maybe Kravtsov was born to recent settlers who would soon be forced into a collective farm. Second, starting in 1920, Ukrainians arrived in mass deportations. Maybe his parents (his mother, at least) were deported to Kazakhstan in the 1920-22 Ukrainian famine.

Starvation would stalk Kazakhstan, too. Kazakh crops were seized in the 1920s to feed other parts of the Soviet Union and for export. Soon, the great Kazakh famine of 1930-1933 would kill around one-fourth (a million-plus people) of the republic. In 1933, at age 11, Kravtsov was already being put to work on a collective farm. *[111]*

After Kravtsov's father died, the family endured rural Soviet life in the 1920s and 1930s—famines, grain confiscations, arrests, deportations, collectivization, shortages, arbitrary rule, disease epidemics, church closures, the rise of labor camps, orphan crime, homeless people, cannibalism. Then Kravtsov was sent off to die.

"Glory to the heroes!" with faked aviator image

Kravtsov's mother and relatives, May 1945

The absurd official story is that he entered the war as a pilot but volunteered as a **SMERSH** lieutenant in a front-line punishment unit. The life expectancy of a penal unit officer was several months at best. Why would the Army transfer a scarce, expensively-trained pilot from the cockpit into one of the worst jobs of all—cannon fodder?

We don't know what really happened to Kravtsov. Maybe he started in an aviation-related program but caused problems and landed in a penal company. Maybe he was assigned to the battalion as a conscripted exile. Maybe airplanes were never really any part of this unfortunate young man's story at all.

His stamp and Hero poster reinforce the absurdity of the lie. The two aviators are fakes, with a pilot's cap and goggles added to drawings based on an earlier photo. The poster says nothing about aviation.

We can believe a part of Kravtsov's story: he died a terrible death on 14 January 1945 in Poland. From contemporary accounts we know that mid-January temperatures in the area that year were nearly forty degrees below zero. Conditions were terrible for regular army units, and worse for penal units like Kravtsov's. They were considered more expendable and thus often had poor equipment, and less of it (clothing, weapons, food, and so on). Typically they attacked on foot in advance of regular units. Kravtsov's penal unit went up against a German emplacement on the far side of the frozen Vistula River. He may have been hit by an artillery shell as the official report claimed, or he may have stepped on a landmine. We will never know whether the explosive that blew this boy into pieces was German or Soviet.

In late April, a few weeks after what would have Kravtsov's twenty-third birthday, his mother learned that her son had been designated a Hero and would never return home. A few days later she sat for a publicity photo with some family children and a daughter-in-law. No one smiled. *[91, 92, 93, 111, 112]*

Mikhail Sergeevich Kedrov

Mikhail Sergeevich Kedrov of the VCheka's Special Department we have already met as murderer and co-founder of the Gulag.

His stamp is a lie. He had no armored train. He requested one for Arkhangelsk but was denied.

Still, the stamp's irony is perfect—Kedrov's mythical train cannon takes aim at Kedrov himself.

Trains took him to Switzerland, where he learned medicine and a doctor's traditional Hippocratic Oath. Trains took him to Vologda and Arkhangelsk, where he killed people and opened concentration camps. They took him to Tambov and the Caspian, where he continued deadly revolutionary justice. And, in the end, trains took Kedrov to his doom.

"Live by the train, die by the train" could have been his epitaph, but he has no gravestone.

Kedrov's stamp is an ideal postal metaphor for the entire Soviet-Chekist-Russian experiment: suspicion, violence, self-deception, and self-destruction. Recall the appalling "game" called Russian roulette, in which a player points a revolver loaded with one round at his own head and pulls the trigger, hoping to fire on an empty chamber. In the Soviet version, the Cheka was not a revolver but a semi-automatic pistol—every pull of the trigger was deadly. The Soviet Union could not put this gun down and over the course of seven decades, the system slowly killed itself.

Artistic blunder or deliberate subversion, it doesn't matter. We must honor the daring depiction of the circular nature of Lenin's revolutionary justice.

Peter Anfimovich Zhidkov

Peter Anfimovich Zhidkov (1904-1943) was a Russian counterintelligence officer in an army tank unit. He was from a poor family in Ivanovo, an industrial city northeast of Moscow. At age 15, during the Civil War, he found jobs to help feed his seven siblings. He had various jobs over the next few years—shoemaker, railway, textile mill. In 1936 he landed a job in the propaganda newspaper office of the large Zhideleva textile mill in his home city. The fate of his parents and siblings is not known.

Drafted in 1941, he took NKVD courses and was sent to Ukraine in 1942 as a counterintelligence officer in engineering and tank units. Apparently his stamp's armored car is meant to evoke this.

He died in Khotov, a village near Kyiv, during the brutal battle of November 1943. In 1948 his wife Ekaterina Efimovna was notified he was a Hero of the Soviet Union. This may have been the first time she was told he was dead.

Zhidkov has long been memorialized as a local hero in Ivanovo. The city has numerous memorials for the many residents who were killed in the war. Zhidkov's name is on almost half a dozen monuments and plaques—from an old one at School No. 38 to more recent ones. And, the Russian government made images of his field-written award file publicly available. *[95, 96, 97]*

Interestingly, someone has digitally censored one or two lines of text on the front page of Zhidkov's award file. There is a perfectly blank rectangle on the left side just below midway. The color match is close but not perfect, and parts are missing from the paper's guidelines. The content of the censored lines is unknown.

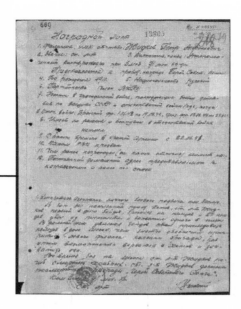

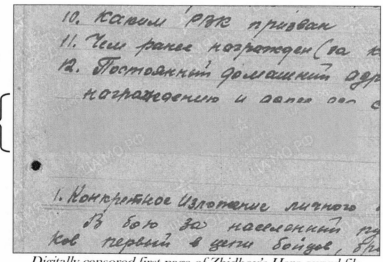

Digitally-censored first page of Zhidkov's Hero award file, field-written 14 Nov 1943   [97]

Vasily Mikhailovich Chebotarev

Vasily Mikhailovich Chebotarev (1918-44) was born 25 June 1918, during the Bolshevik takeover of Kazakhstan, in tiny Gavrilovka, two hundred miles east of fellow stamp man Grigory Kravtsov's village.

Chebotarev's stamp isn't a lie, but it is deceptive.

He survived the repeated Kazakh famines. He began working as a teenager, first on the Khleborob (Breadman) state farm then in a mine. At twenty, he entered the army, became a sniper, and spent more than a year near Leningrad (including two horrific winters). After NKVD training, he was sent to the front again, this time as a counterintelligence officer in Belarus.

He was a strong young man, and we can believe that he was a brave soldier. Many of his fellow troops died, and so did he. At the Bobr River, his unit was ordered to advance into heavily armed German positions. There were tanks, but Chebotarev was part of an infantry group moving on foot toward German guns.

As with many Soviet advances, the results were predictable—an outnumbered and ill-protected unit was thrown forward and wiped out, to be replaced by another unit, and yet another. Perhaps we could refer to this standard Soviet cannon-fodder approach to offensive operations as the "Red Wave" style of warfare.

His official stories hint at the Kremlin's disregard for the lives of individual troops. Chebotarev inspired his tank unit, he held a hilltop for a day, he killed many Germans, he captured the turncoat SS Lieutenant Ryaglikov, he tried to save 18-year-old field nurse Maria Inkina. The retreating Nazis even took time to defile his corpse with numerous stab wounds and a Soviet star cut into his chest (just like stamp man Krygin, whom we will meet below).

The official record says Chebotarev was killed 27 June 1944 (two days after he turned twenty-six). A SMERSH officer says he buried the young man on the side of a road 2500 kilometers from home. He became a Hero of the Soviet Union in 1945. *[98, 99]*

His biography from the Belarus MVD states he had a wife Evdokia and a daughter Elena. A local museum in Belarus apparently has an extensive exhibit of personal correspondence and other related items, which might shed light on the family's fate.

As noted earlier, two days before his LPR stamp Chebotarev was placed on a Russian sheet. The inscription refers to his Hero of the Soviet Union award for his exemplary performance of combat missions of command at the front, courage and heroism shown in battles during Operation Bagration [the 1944 Belarus offensive]. The background is Soviet blood-red.

The Germans killed more than a million civilians in Belarus.

However, before the Germans arrived—and after they retreated—the Soviets destroyed or deported hundreds of thousands more.

Viktor Abakumov's arrest photos, 1951

Viktor Semenovich Abakumov (1908-54), head of **SMERSH**, claimed in a personnel document that he was born to a day-laborer and a seamstress/nurse, attended four years of school, joined a "special purpose" Communist unit, and became a "packer" (упаковщик) in the Moscow Union of Industrial Cooperation. An official investigation in 1952 could not corroborate this story, so we do not know the real tale. His managerial skill and writing suggest he was better educated than he admitted.

He joined the OGPU in the early 1930s. His bosses soon noticed that he was less interested in the details of Marxist-Leninist theory and more interested in meeting prisoners' wives and other women for afternoon liaisons. For his political illiteracy and sexual debauchery, Abakumov was demoted to the Gulag camp division, but soon he moved out of camp management and up to the secret department, where he built a reputation for rape, torture, and executions. He helped carry out the Great Purge for Yezhov, then shifted loyalty to Beria when Yezhov was shot. When Germany invaded, he helped Stalin scapegoat and kill Red Army officers, then built **SMERSH** for political control of the rapidly-growing armed forces.

At war's end Abakumov sent hundreds of thousands of returning soldiers and former POWs to Gulag camps. In 1946 he became Minister of State Security. In his most artful post-war act, Abakumov helped fabricate the "Leningrad Affair". More than two thousand city residents, who survived nearly nine hundred days of siege and starvation and the wretched aftermath, were sent off to camps or shot.

Abakumov fell from grace in another, less successful fabrication, the "Doctors' Plot", a stumbling, evolving project to arrest educated Jews, doctors, and others in a scheme which never gained the official momentum or rabid energy of earlier Chekist plots. Saboteurs, spies, and assassins had been unmasked more than two decades, and the idea was just worn out. Unfortunately for Abakumov, Beria was no longer a patron but a rival who imprisoned Abakumov in 1951 along with his wife and infant son.

His arrest photos are less impressive than his stamp. We must rememember that most arrests were done late at night, when neither prisoners nor photographers were at their best. Abakumov's face is puffy but not beaten—the fault lies in shadows cast by a poorly-placed light. The beatings would begin later. He certainly was tough. After three and a half years of abuse, he still refused to confess. His wife and nearly-four-year-old son were released several days before his demise. On 19 December 1954, he was shot.

The Abakumovs had already lost their Moscow mansion. KGB investigators cataloged, removed, and enjoyed a trove of stolen German items—furniture, art, shoes, wristwatches, even a car.

By the way, it also is safe to presume that a large quantity of still-missing European artwork, including art stolen from Jews by the Nazis, wound up on the walls of powerful Soviet officials and in our present day is hidden away in the houses of powerful Russians.

Abakumov's widow and son took her maiden surname. Antonina Nikolaevna Smirnova lost her job as a state security official.

Son Igor Viktorovich Smirnov built a scientific career doing, of all things, mind-control experiments. Perhaps they worked—in the 1990s, he succeeded in having his father rehabilitated. Twice. Russian courts retroactively downgraded the charges against Viktor Abakumov, and then reduced the proper punishment.

Besides his new stamp, Abakumov enjoys positive treatment in the one and only Gulag campsite which Russia has made into an official museum. The Perm-36 museum opened as a site of solemn remembrance. It now has been revamped to normalize the Gulag by highlighting the contributions of prison slave-workers to war and the economy. *[100, 103]*

Stamp man Viktor Abakumov was an avaricious killer. To see how his official portrait is being been polished beyond recognition, one need only visit the shiny new black granite Abakumov family grave, complete with graven images of father, mother, and son in the Rakitki cemetery on the outskirts of Moscow. It was installed in 2013, clearly with the support of the government of Vladimir Putin.

Mikhail Petrovich Krygin

Mikhail Petrovich Krygin (18 July 1918-13 August 1945), like stamp men Kravtsov and Chebotarev, came from farmlands: in his case Kabanovka village, next to a Samara region rail line. His stamp is, of course, deceptive.

Krygin became fatherless in the mid-1930s, just as the Cheka's Gulag gates were swinging wide open. His father's death is not explained, whether ordinary, or starvation, execution or camp. The fates of his mother and siblings are unknown.

Krygin became a typesetter. Drafted in 1939, he went as a junior naval political officer to the busy eastern port of Vladivostok. In 1943, Krygin took **NKVD** courses to become a **SMERSH** officer. His years of work in Vladivostok are not documented but he would have helped monitor crews of the many American Lend-Lease supply ships and the Soviet Gulag fleet which took prisoners to Kolyma camps and brought back the products of their labor. *[177]*

The Soviets depended on American supplies but stayed neutral toward Japan and contributed nothing to the war against it. However, on 13 August 1945, two days before the war ended, the Soviets declared war on lost-cause Japan and seized the Japanese-occupied Korean port city of Chongjin (Seisin, in Russian). Barely 150 miles south of Vladivostok, Chongjin was under severe Japanese rule.

This last-minute attack cost young Krygin his life. It began not with a giant naval ship as suggested by his stamp, but with a reconnaissance group in torpedo boats. Krygin's unit may have been paratroopers as one source claims (the Soviets were obsessed with parachute propaganda), but they arrived in boats. *[114]*

Outnumbered, Krygin's detachment was wiped out. The main Soviet landing force arrived three days later and soon overran the city. They found Krygin's body and others who remain unnamed.

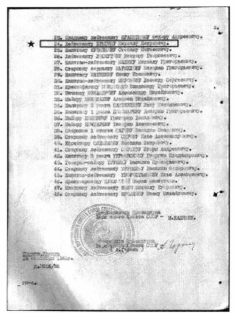

Lieutenant Krygin, No. 24 on the
14 September 1945 Hero decree list

Like Kravtsov and Chebotarev, Krygin was expended in a small forward unit thrown against stronger opposing forces. In Krygin's case, though, it seems his unit was sent in merely so the Soviets could claim the battle had already started and were thus entitled to occupy the city and establish order, even though the war was technically over.

The records of the event are confusing. He may have been left behind, or commanded a small group while another retreated. Soviet tales are self-serving and truth is difficult to discern. We do know that regular armed forces generally detested **SMERSH**. Maybe Krygin was thus chosen for a risky job, or tasked with a sacrificial defense.

His death record reads like it was written by Vasily Chebotarev's obituarist. The two Heros received identical defilement—numerous bayonet wounds and a star cut into the chest. Regardless of the truth of the event and his death, the Soviets added further insult by burying Krygin in a mass grave under one of Chongjin's streets. Even at war's end, in an attack close to a home port, he and the other young men who died there, perhaps the last Soviet battle deaths in the war, were not brought home or given individual graves. *[101, 114]*

Just like Chebotarev, Krygin was put on a blood-red Russian stamp two days before appearing in the **LPR**. The sheet notes his Hero award for fearlessness and heroism in the fight against the Japanese invaders during the Seisin operation. It says nothing about the personal truth of his life: he grew up in starvation times, lost his father, worked in a distant city filled with Gulag prisoners, and was buried under a Korean street soon after his twenty-seventh birthday.

The Soviets called the Chongjin attack "liberation". Soon they would give the city to the Communists of Kim Il-Sung's new Democratic People's Republic of Korea for more liberation. Presumably Krygin still rests beneath the Korean Workers' Paradise.

Rails of remembrance

It is hard to feel sympathy for 2018's stamp men Kedrov and Abakumov. They were mature, politically powerful men. Kedrov was born well-off, Abakumov poor, but both spent years rising to high levels by enabling the Cheka's "merciless fight". They used positional power to inflict their operational and administrative decisions on people with little power to fight back—civilians, prisoners, soldiers.

In contrast, Kravtsov, Chebotarev, Krygin, and Zhidkov deserve sympathetic remembrance for dismal childhoods and violent deaths.

Their official stories may or may not be true. Their stamps do not honor their human individuality. The four Heroes mattered to the Cheka and the Soviet government as propaganda. They died truly terrible deaths, but became faces and names for posters, monuments, and tales of the country's salvation by a heroic army and the secret police. They died, their brief lives were briefly noted, and then they were mostly forgotten until their postal resurrection

We don't know how they lived and behaved or what they felt and believed. They may have become good men or bad, and may have acted with dignity or ignobility. We do know that they grew up in a nation washed again and again by red waves of famine and terror. In the end they had little choice but to fight and die for the rulers who had spawned such misery. They spent their entire lives in a cruel system, and were made to die to preserve it.

Whatever they believed or did or became, they once were children, and children are fascinated by trains.

Railroads were quite literally the Bolsheviks' circulatory system. Trains moved the nutritional energy of grain and industrial materials throughout the Soviet empire. Trains moved boxcars of red blood

Railroad winter work: Prisoners laying wooden "sleepers".
(Contemporary uncopyrighted photo)

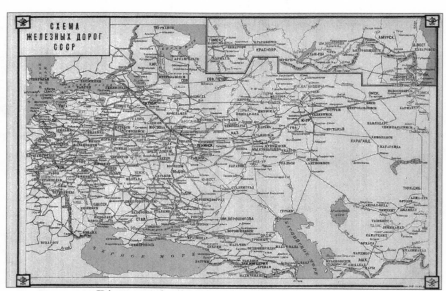

Diagram of railways of the USSR, early 1940s.
(Contemporary uncopyrighted photo)

cells—prisoners to camps and soldiers to the front in the Bolsheviks' various wars. Trains also carried leukocyte Chekists to destroy any anti-Soviet infection. An unfortunate metaphorical irony arises. Red Chekists were the white blood cells seeking out the Civil War's White Russians (anti-Bolsheviks) to destroy them in order to protect the Reds. Unfortunately, the antibiotic Chekists were not very discriminating, and engulfed many red-blooded Soviets as well.

As a boy, Mikhail Krygin saw boxcars rattling westward with the Samara region's agricultural produce to feed the great cities of Russia, and boxcars rolling east filled with human beings to re-infuse Siberian labor camps, which consumed live blood at a prodigious rate. The nearby city Samara was a major transfer site in the Gulag system.

While young Krygin watched trains, five or six hundred miles due east in Kazakhstan young Kravtsov and Chebotarev did the same. They saw trains arrive with starving exiles from Ukraine and other places to invigorate Soviet agriculture with fresh but thin blood, and watched trains depart for Russia loaded with Kazakh grain and livestock while Kazakhstan starved during collectivization.

Zhidkov, only a few years older, also watched similar trains pass through his industrial town near Moscow. The railroad through Ivanovo was a branch of the mainline to the north—perhaps as a teenager Zhidkov saw Mikhail Kedrov's train pass by.

Two decades later as the red rose of war again budded, blossomed and bled, all four of the young stamp men watched trains of drafted farm boys and factory workers packed into railcars heading off to fight and die in unfamiliar, faraway places. Soon enough, Kravtsov, Chebotarev, Krygin and Zhidkov would join them.

.

11. How much blood?

More blood, as much blood as possible.
"Blood for Blood", <u>Red Gazette</u>, 1 September 1918 [121]

ESTIMATES VARY widely of deaths caused by the Cheka and the Soviets in general from 1917 until Stalin's death, an event which marked a shift away from the remarkable rate of self-exsanguination that characterized the Soviet Union for more than three decades. The newspaper quote above, from a Civil War editorial, emphasizes that bloody enforcement was official policy from the very beginning.

We will *exclude* the roughly twenty million Soviet citizens who died during World War II, or the Great Patriotic War as the Soviets dubbed it. If we count *only* deaths from execution, collectivization, deportation, famine, and camps from 1917 through the early 1950s, the Soviets themselves calculated a number roughly equal to war deaths—that is, twenty million. *[102]*

Of course, this number is debatable. The Cheka and its successors did not commit all of these deaths but they did play a central role. They defined, enabled, operated, and expanded the systems, structures, and mindset that caused these deaths.

The average human body contains around five liters of blood. Five times twenty million is 100,000,000 liters of blood.

The rate of flow of a modern bath shower-head is around 7.6 liters (2 gallons) per minute. The uninterrupted flow of one hundred million liters of blood through one shower-head would last more than twenty-five years.

12. Epilogue: The right of correspondence

Truth seldom is pleasant.
Alexander Solzhenitsyn *[182]*

IMAGINE THE FACE of Heinrich Mueller, head of Hitler's Gestapo, on a modern German stamp. Imagine a new stamp from Cambodia with a portrait of Kang Kek Iew, chief of the Khmer Rouge's prison camps in the late 1970s. Imagine new United States stamps featuring Civil War prisoner-of-war camp commanders, or Bull Connor, the Alabama official who in 1963 ordered fire hoses and attack dogs to be used on citizen protesters.

Do we wish, regardless of who or where we are, to find pride in history? Of course—we are human. Does a nation want to move forward, put the past to rest? Certainly, that is natural.

Is it dangerous to misunderstand the continuing influence of a painful history? This is the most important question. Even Stalin quoted the Bible (Ezekiel 18:20) to note that the sins of one generation should not be visited upon the next, but he was disingenuous—his victims' families were punished severely.

Indeed, if a brutal sin is repeated, pervasive, and institutional, its consequences are necessarily visited on the future—consequences are long-lived and destructive when the wish to forget is overwhelming. Lenin's central crime, the Cheka and its innumerable stamp men, has affected Russia for more than a century. The crime is detected even in (seemingly) simple postage stamps. Putin's Boys—the 2002 and

2018 stamp men—are cases of self-inflicted postal amnesia. They keep alive the Soviet propensity to euphemize or euthanize history and to minimize or simply erase unhelpful truths, particularly regarding the Cheka and its successors: "Every effort has been made to confuse these events." *[159, p. 21]*

Perhaps these stern Chekist stamp men, embellished photographs of young men, are meant to inspire or warn. Their stories, however, betray wishful thinking and ignorance, self-deception and destructive suspicion, and weakness and insecurity born of a painful past.

Kedrov and his nephew Artuzov co-founded the Gulag. Demidenko kidnapped people. Olsky killed people. Puzitsky sent hundreds of thousands of people into exile. Styrne watched people starve. Syroezhkin beat people to death. Abakumov tortured people and terrorized his country's army. Kravtsov, Zhidkov, Chebotarev, and Krygin were some of Abakumov's agents.

The stamp men are official lies, a disease which damages the very heart of society and can make us unable to discern truth.

Let us look at four brief examples of the relationship between individuals and truth. One is new, three we have already met.

First, let us take meet ***Tamara Makarova*** (1907-1997), a Soviet actress who, with her director husband Sergei Gerasimov, thrived with a stream of propagandistic films. In <u>Komsomolsk</u> (1938), for example, a volunteer youth labor-army builds a new shipyard city. In reality, Gulag inmates donated much of the back-breaking labor to create the new industrial port. The film adds brief borrowed footage to celebrate the launch of a new ship *Komsomolsk*. In reality, the ship was built and launched in 1936 in an English shipyard. Some historians believe it was used in the far eastern Gulag in 1940. *[177]*

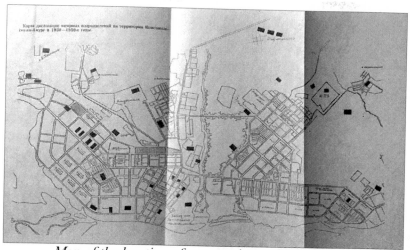

Map of the location of camp units on the territory of
Komsomolsk-na-Amure in the years 1930-1950. [181]

Komsomolsk helped Makarova and her husband, but with a price. Many of their colleagues were shot or sent to camp. When Tamara's own sister Lyudmila and brother-in-law Adolf Tsivilko were arrested, she adopted their children Artur and Emma. Artur was murdered in 1995. In her post-Soviet interviews and memoirs, Makarova avoided discussing the past. Ten years after she died, she was put on a stamp.

Second, recall **Boris Gudz**, the Chekist-turned-bus-driver who burnished his tales in interviews. Perhaps he wanted to redeem himself by portraying Artuzov as the consummate, dedicated "clean hands" Chekist. But, even in old age he was alienated from his surviving siblings and former brother-in-law, and would not mention them or their suffering. He enjoyed interviews and awards, and slept well enough at night to live more than a century.

Third, consider **Bonifati Kedrov**, Artuzov's Chekist cousin. The Cheka killed his father, brother, two cousins, step-brother's father, foster-brother and wife, and his cousin's second wife, arrested his step-brother, and sent his cousin's son to Kolyma. Little brother Yuri may have committed suicide. Bonifati survived all this to become a chemistry professor whose academic work included attacking scientists. Was he a true believer or an opportunist? Perhaps he was being denounced by colleagues, terrified that he and his remaining loved ones would suffer if he did not amplify the Party line.

Finally, what are we to make of Bonifati's step-brother *Vladimir Plastinin*? A Chekist interrogator until his 1939 arrest, he avoided a Gulag death and witnessed the same family deaths as Bonifati. Thirty years later in 1969 Vladimir did a most surprising thing. He wrote a tribute to Mikhail Kedrov, the father figure who had pulled them all into this mess. The book was cited in Smirnov's panegyric collection of essays about Kedrov two decades later. *[133]*

Maybe Vladimir believed his step-father's official hagiography as a brilliant Old Bolshevik who repelled anti-Communist invaders and brought Soviet freedom to Arkhangelsk. Perhaps he needed to confirm the validity of his own life. Who can say?

These four examples—Tamara Makarova's reluctance to talk, Boris Gudz's fabrications, Bonifati Kedrov's destructiveness, and Vladimir Plastinin's book—show a deeply-rooted reluctance to discuss the truth of the past and to reveal feelings, participation, knowledge. Myths and lies can be more comfortable, but they make speculation a necessary part of the search for truth when we look at events and people connected to the Cheka.

Putin's Russia is not the only place we find this disease. Many countries—and many people—have hidden pasts. Some pasts are covered with wind-blown sand and the vicissitudes of fading memory and time. Other pasts are concealed by mud and stone, submerged underwater or buried underground, guideposts and maps torn down and burned.

Still, our pasts remain. In time, sands may blow away, waters may recede, and soils may erode to reveal secrets and test our beliefs, but we cannot put our faith in circumstance to uncover the truth—we must make our own efforts, and involve new generations.

A wonderful example is a 2014 school survey about the significance of street names. An Arkhangelsk teenager asked 172 of her schoolmates to identify Mikhail Kedrov. Less than half knew. When they learned what he did in their city, two-thirds agreed that Kedrov Street should be renamed (one-fourth thought it was too expensive or unimportant). The student's teacher thought the project was important enough to post it online three years later. *[163]*

Russia can be a healthy home for its people, an outstanding place for business, and the highly admired political actor it should be on the international stage. To do so will require a more open self-appraisal, a healthy dose of Gorbachev's "self-critical optimism".

Russia must correspond truthfully with by writing honest letters, in large and official ways. In the late 1980s and early 1990s, the country began to do this at many levels, with difficult conversations and newly opened files. Unfortunately, the stamp men make clear that honesty remains an inconvenience for the highest levels of government.

Many of the victims are lost to time in unknown graves. The camps have been dismantled. The railroad cars and prisoner convoy ships were scrapped decades ago. The enormous construction projects—cities, buildings, canals, roads, railways, dams, subways— remain, but give little sense of those who suffered to create them.

In 1954-1955, millions of government files representing three and a half decades of secret police activity were destroyed: office files, investigation files, employee files, foreign intelligence files, files on citizens, files on foreigners, and on and on.

"Cleaning" out the archives became a routine administrative function until the 1991 collapse of the Soviet Union. Vladimir Putin himself destroyed KGB files in East Germany.

After the early 1990s when some remaining archives became more accessible, the newly named FSB reasserted dominance over what constitutes truth by restricting archival access, limiting transfers of records to external depositories, and resuming the destruction of evidence. As Petrov (2001) observed, "concealment of history is the main aspect of national Russian politics...a characteristic feature of a resurgent police state." [168, 169]

And, now, to continue to re-write and legitimize the past, Vladimir Putin is destroying one of the remaining mountains of proof of the particular tragedies of millions of prisoners. The archival record of the past is not just locked away—it is being obliterated.

In 2014 the Russian Ministry of Internal Affairs received a classified order to destroy decades of Gulag file cards that documented names, dates, camp transfers, and fates (e.g., death, release, exile). In the city of Magadan, headquarters of the horrific Kolyma camps, the records have been destroyed, as they probably have been in many other places by now. [71]

This permanent erasure of the past is worse than concealment. When scarce information about parents, grandparents, and ancestors is consigned to oblivion, we are left adrift in time, ignorant of our identity, unable to learn why we exist, incapable of comprehending anything about those who came before us, or that they ever walked the earth at all. Putin seems unworried about condemning his own descendants to exist in historical ignorance.

We now arrive at the bleak central irony of the stamp men.

If a victim's family members were not pulled into the Cheka's currents as well by association, or mass exile, or resettlement, sometimes they were told the truth about a person's fate. There might have been a trial of some sort and a guilty verdict, followed by a death sentence, or internal exile, or prison, or hard labor. Many families, however, were told their relatives were imprisoned "without the right of correspondence", unable to send or receive letters or parcels through the mail. In truth, their loved ones were already dead.

For those victims who remained alive in camps or in exile, there was little privacy in which to write honest letters about their experiences, conditions, and sentiments. We can still read the Cheka's detailed procedures used by a formidably extensive administration to open any or all of the nation's mail. *[33]*

The stamp men's victims had, thus, no need of stamps.

"Ni shagu nazad!" Iissued in 1945 to commemorate Stalin's infamous "Not one step back" 1942 Order No. 227, which created penal battalions like Grigory Kravtsov's unit. To prevent retreat and encourage advance, the order also formed blocking detachments to point Soviet guns at the backs of Soviet soldiers.

APPENDIX

Russia today: 160+ Chekist stamps

IN ADDITION TO the 2002 and 2018 stamp men, post-Soviet Russia has a flood of stamps with Chekist secret police connections. Our non-exhaustive list *excludes* many stamps about weapons and wars, regions and political relationships. These 1992-2019 stamps illustrate the pervasive yet often hidden or forgotten role of the secret police, and are organized into five categories:

Infrastructure and projects—built by or related to prisoners

Bureaucracy—agencies and units connected to the secret police

Chekists—employees and agents

Victims—individuals, or their relatives or colleagues

Miscellaneous

Before moving to the stamps themselves, we should note that the issue rate of new Cheka-connected stamps is rising, from a couple per year in the early 1990s, to dozens in 2018-2019.

Infrastructure and projects

1992 Moscow State University. In 1949-1953, thousands of Gulag prisoners built the main skyscraper building.

1995 Peter & Paul Fortress, a St. Petersburg site where archaeologists verified Cheka mass graves in 2010.

1999 M1A motorcycle, introduced in 1946 using an entire DKW motorcycle factory stolen from Germany. The KGB kidnapped workers to reassemble and restart the factory.

2002 Trans-Siberian Railway, which transported millions of exiles and prisoners.

2002 population census, which was conducted in a normal manner but can bring to mind the disastrous 1937 Soviet census.

2003 <u>Historical Russian automobiles</u>, including the GAZ-M1, built in a 1930s production line bought from Henry Ford. American experts came to set up the factory for kit-car assembly then manufacturing. The Cheka sent some Americans to the Gulag, but the US government did little. Similarly, the US did little for US citizens who moved to the Soviet Union, or individuals who had come to the US but left during the Great Depression for Soviet promises. Many of these cases had the worst possible ending. For example, Emil Grinevich left western Ukraine for the US then returned to the Soviet Union around 1932, found work in a car repair shop, and was shot in 1937. *[205, 206]*

2004 <u>Baikonur Cosmodrome</u> launch facility in Kazakhstan. To mislead the West, it was named for a town more than 150 miles away. The region had been home to various Gulag mining camps.

2005 <u>Moscow Metro</u> Seventieth anniversary of the opening of the first line of the subway system, built largely by **NKVD** prisoners.

2006 <u>Arktikugol Trust</u>—a Gulag coal-mine camp on the Arctic island of Svalbard, now a state-owned enterprise. In early years it was run by the father of Maya Plisetskaya (see her 2017 stamp).

2007 <u>Russian Academy of Economics named for Georgi Plekhanov</u>. Plekhanov was an early Marxist economist with very hostile relationships with Lenin and the Bolsheviks. He left Russia in 1917 and moved a few miles into Finland to a village which is now a suburb of St. Petersburg. He died in 1918, supposedly of tuberculosis. Lenin's enmity is ample reason to wonder if the Cheka killed him. His name was put on the Karl Marx Institute in 1924 soon after Lenin died, a move that would have appealed to Stalin's sense of humor.

2009 Solovetsky Islands, the "mother tumor" of the Gulag system, in Solzhenitsyn's words.

2010 Watches. Flush with cash from grain exports, in 1930 the USSR bought and shipped two US watch/clock factories to Moscow. In 1935 the factory was named for Sergei Kirov, whom the Cheka killed the previous year for Stalin.

2014 Baikal-Amur Railway. Commonly known as BAM, construction began with Gulag prisoners, was interrupted by WWII, then renewed in the 1970s under Brezhnev.

2015 Norilsk Nickel, the Putin-friendly oligarch-owned firm which now owns Norilsk, an Arctic mine city built and run for decades by Gulag prisoners. Many current resident-employees are descendants of prisoners   Norilsk is the most polluted city in Russia and the single biggest sulfur-dioxide polluter in the world.

2016 Lukoil, one of the world's biggest oil producers, was formed from old Soviet oil production, processing, and distribution entities. The Cheka and successors greatly expanded oil/coal/gas activity in the North and elsewhere—fpr decades, camp inmates built infrastructure where none existed, then operated the mines and wells. The modern profits of Putin-oriented Lukoil are rooted in Gulag slave labor.

2018 Moscow Metro art. Prisoners built and decorated the initial system, overseen partly by Nikita Khruschchev.

2019 Moscow Metro, more political art, mostly modern, in the metro.

2019 Moscow's Exhibition of Achievements of the National Economy (previously known as the All-Union Agricultural Exhibition), a monumental propaganda park which opened in 1939 after years of delay in which various managers and architects were shot or sent off to camp.

Bureaucracy

 **1996 GAI**, the traffic police, created in 1936 as part of NKVD, which controlled road construction and used prison labor.

 **2000 Foreign intelligence agency**, 80th anniversary of the founding of the Cheka's foreign intelligence unit.

 **2003 Novosibirsk**, major railway city which depended for decades on Gulag—home to several camp administrations, transfer prisons, prison industries, and local camp systems.

 **2003 Russian journalism tricentennial.** Soviet news was state-controlled; journalists were censored and/or repressed by the Cheka.

 2004 ITAR-TASS, state-run news agency often used as a cover for Chekists doing foreign intelligence work.

 **2015 The Dzerzhinsky Division**, the ODON (Separate Operational Assignment Division), is a century-old armored "special forces" unit of Chekists for domestic use by the internal affairs ministry. Their motto? "Any time, any place, any task!"

2017 Procurator General of the Russian Federation. The office of the nation's top prosecutor, notable mostly for its century of Chekists, terror and, more recently, corruption.

We can review the history of Soviet and Russian chief prosecutors. Peter Krasikov (in office 1924-33) previously helped run the Red Terror as co-chairman of the Petrograd Cheka, and ran an anti-religion campaign which included killing priests and seizing church valuables. Ivan Akulov (1933-35) was previously deputy chair of the OGPU; he was shot in 1937. Andrei Vyshinsky (1935-39) purged Moscow University, ran show trials of innocents, and created the "no evidence is necessary" legal foundation for the Great Purge. Mikhail I. Pankratiev (1939-40) signed endless execution orders but was pushed after butting heads with Beria.

Viktor Bochkov (1940-43) before becoming procurator worked almost 17 years for the OGPU/NKVD, including running the prison division and the secret division; after the procurator job he helped run the 1944 mass deportations of Chechens and others, and was deputy chief of GULAG. Bochkov also is the official who fabricated post-mortem paperwork to authorize the 1941 execution of Mikhail Kedrov and two dozen others., and who used tanks to suppress the 1954 Kengir/Steplag camp rebellion. *[233]*

Konstantin Gorshenin (1943-48) secretly approved death sentences and participated in the notorious Gulag imprisonment of German POWs. Grigory Savonov (1948-53) began as a prosecutor under Vyshinsky and was removed from office four days after Beria's arrest. Roman Rudenko (1953-81) has a personal 2015 stamp. He condemned thousands in the Great Terror, ran the NKVD Special Camp No. 7 where more than 12,000 died, and shot a Vorkuta mine inmate in the head. Alexander Rekunkov (1981-88) entered the Tbilisi Artillery School as a youth in 1939, presumably to help enforce Soviet order after 40,000 Georgians had been killed in the preceding two years. Alexander Sukharev (1988-90) had worked for more than a decade at Komsomol, which had close ties to the secret police and provided at least two KGB chiefs. <u>Nikolai Trubin</u> (1990-92) worked in the 1950s as prosecutor of the Pechora forced labor camp. <u>Valentin Stepankov</u> (1991-93, the) first procurator of post-Soviet Russia, arrested KGB chief Kryuchkov and others for their coup attempt against Gorbachev. <u>Aleksei Kazannik</u> (1993-94) was a reformist but lasted only six months. <u>Alexei Ilyushenko</u> (1994-95) was fired and charged with corruption relating to sale of state assets. <u>Oleg Gaidanov</u> (1995) was interim procurator for two weeks. <u>Yuri Skuratov</u> (1995-2000) was fired when he opened corruption cases against high government officials; he accused Vladimir Putin of killing the cases and forcing him out by creating *kompromat* sex tapes of Skuratov. <u>Vladimir Ustinov</u> (2000-06) prosecuted the Yukos Oil/Khodorkovsky oligarch case for Putin, which helped convert other Russian oligarchs to Putin loyalists. <u>Yuri Chaika</u> (2006-present) has two sons who have become extremely wealthy since their father became chief procurator. Chaika himself owns a 17,000 square foot house outside Moscow and had a long history of financial corruption, sometimes intermingled with the KGB/FSB. *[232]*

<u>2018 The Sergo Ordzhonikidze command school</u>, named for Stalin's long-time, close friend who died by gunshot, possibly suicide. The NKVD killed many of Orzhonokidze's family or sent them to the camps.

<u>2018 Komsomol</u>, the Communist Youth League, which developed ideologically suitable managerial cadres and was fertile ground to recruit new Chekist informers.

<u>2018 The Kurchatov Institute</u>, which began as Beria's NKVD atomic bomb lab. Worker mortality from digging uranium ore in Gulag mines approached 100%. Namesake I.V. Kurchatov had his own stamp in 2003.

Chekists

<u>1998 Leontina and Morris Koen</u> (Cohen), American citizens, worked as NKVD/KGB spies, fled the US in 1950.

<u>1998 Leonid Krasnikov and Anatoly Yatskov</u>, NKVD/KGB agents in New York, managed Cohens and other spies.

<u>2000 Vladimir Putin</u>, new president of the Russian Federation, former KGB agent.

<u>2002 Counterintelligence,</u> The stamp men.

<u>2012 Marina Raskova</u>, pilot and half–sister of Boris Malinin (repressed engineer, 1993 stamp). In 1943 Raskova flew into winter weather conditions and crashed. In 1937-1941 she worked for the NKVD.

<u>2012 Vladimir Putin</u>, president of the Russian Federation, former KGB agent.

2013 Heydar Aliyev, career Chekist (Azerbaijan NKGB), then president of Azerbaijan. (In St. Petersburg there is a plaque at 6 Gorokhovaya Street, where Aliyev went to state security school, a one-minute walk to stamp man Syroezhkin's old office building.

2013 Sergei Mikhailkov, popular author of children's books and lyric-writer for the Soviet / Russian national anthem. He helped the KGB, and his brother was a KGB agent.

2015 Alexander Galushkin, counterintelligence officer, died 1942 in Crimea after an unsuccessful and undersized landing in Yevpatoria, a German-occupied port. His public biography calls him a career Chekist who died fighting as an NKVD major. Born 1903 in Ivanovka village, (Ivanovo district, Amur region), he was a teenager when the Civil War and Red Terror came to town. Ivanovka's 1916 population was almost 5400; by 1930 it was less than 3000. In 1933 a Mikhail Galushkin from Ivanovka was sent to the camps. *[219, 220]*

2015 Pavel Silaev, NKVD junior political officer in the Black Sea Fleet, born 1916, died 1942. We do not know where or how he survived his first twenty years—his home (Chernukhi village, Poltava region, eastern Ukraine) was ravaged by terror and famine.

2015 Roman Rudenko, prosecutor who condemned thousands as a member of the NKVD troika of the Donetsk region in 1937-38. Later, he was the Soviet prosecutor in the Nuremberg war trials. Until 1950 he was commandant of NKVD Special Camp No. 7, the former German Sachsenhausen camp. Of 60,000-plus prisoners who entered Rudenko's camp, more than 12,000 died. In 1953, he shot a Vorkuta miner. Machine-gunners then shot the rest of the rebelling inmates.

2018 <u>Nikolai Laverov</u>, geologist. Born 1930 in a remote northern village with the rather Bolshevik name of Pozharishche (Conflagration or Fire), likely a deportee settlment. By 2017 its population was five people. In 1955-58 he worked in the "special department" (internal surveillance) of Tsvetmetzoloto, the state entity created in 1930 to oversee Siberian gold-mines (a notorious destination for Gulag prisoners). Tsvetmetzoloto had expanded into uranium—this became Laverov's lifelong specialty. He mapped ore deposits, which means he would have routinely seen Gulag mine camps and countless doomed uranium miners. Perhaps some worked for him.

2018 <u>Alexei Bukhanov</u>, Internal Affairs officer killed in 2003 in Chechnya. In 1944, the NKVD deported 500,000 Chechens and Ingush in less than three weeks.

2018 <u>Alexander Krasikov</u>, FSB officer killed in a brief 2005 rebellion in Kabardino-Balkara. Earlier in 1944 the NKVD deported that republic's entire Balkarian ethnic minority, almost 38,000 people, *in one day.*

2018 <u>Dmitri Gorshkov</u>, Internal Affairs officer killed in 1999 in Dagestan during Chechen fighting. He was from Tula, a city with decades of heavy Chekist presence to watch over the extensive armaments factories and a dense network of regional camps.

2018 <u>inauguration</u> of Vladimir Putin, KGB agent, as president of the Russian Federation.

<u>2018 Counterintelligence</u>, The new stamp men.

<u>2019 Uniforms</u>. At far left is a 1924 OGPU uniform: leather boots, blue pants and the unmistakeable secret policeman's cap—blue top, red band, black visor and gold star.

<u>2019 Oleg Tereshkin</u>, internal affairs ensign, died 1995 in Chechnya. Like Zamaraev (2012 stamp), he was from Sverdlovsk-45 (Lesnoye), a secret uranium-processing city. So, he was likely the descendant of a prisoner, a scientist, or a Chekist.

<u>2019 Roman Kitanin</u>, internal affairs officer killed 2007 in Dagestan, two miles from Chechnya.

<u>2019 Afrika de las Heras</u>, Spanish communist recruited by NKVD. In 1940 she was in Mexico to assist in the killing of Leon Trotsky. She then spent years building spy networks in South America.

<u>2019 Zoya Voskresenskaya-Rybkina</u>, a career Chekist since age 14. Demoted to a camp officer in Vorkuta, she retired and wrote children's stories.

Victims, direct and indirect

1993 Ivan Bubnov, submarine designer, died in Petrograd 13 March 1919, supposedly of typhus. Typhus was common in the city, but there we can question his death. He was a Tsarist official and the son of merchants, both anathema to the Bolsheviks. It is said he died alone in self-imposed quarantine) but that his death was already reported in the newspaper the very next day. Considering that mid-March was a time of violent political crisis in the city, and that the Cheka was busy killing enemies, it seems equally possible that he was murdered, or contracted typhus in prison. At any rate, he died in a capital city in which basic services like water, electricity, sanitation and medical care had collapsed. His wife Anastasia Alexeevna Shapiro-Bubova (b. 1877) died in 1929 of unspecified causes. In 1980 the government moved her grave from a nearby Jewish cemetery and gave the two of them a new joint granite tombstone. The fate of any children is a mystery. *[231]*

1993 Boris Malinin, submarine designer. 1930 death sentence commuted to forced labor.

1993 Pyotr Kapitsa, physicist. He moved to the UK, returned to visit his parents, was denied exit and forced to stay. He spent his life working in NKVD/KGB research institutes. He received more stamps in 2015 and 2019.

1994 Pavel Cherenkov, nuclear physicist, Nobel laureate. Father Alexei Egorovich exiled in 1931, re-arrested 1937, and shot 1938. Father-in-law A. M. Putintsev spent years in Solovki/Svirlag camps, then soon died in Tambov.

1995 Mikhail Fokin, choreographer. Fled Soviet Union and refused to return—many of his theater peers had been denounced, tortured and shot.

1997 Dmitri Shostakovich, composer, endured long bans and restrictions. Many friends and family were arrested, imprisoned, sent to camps, or shot.

1996 Nikolai Semenov, chemist/physicist. He worked against the Bolsheviks in Civil War but somehow avoided the Cheka's waves of arrests in physics and other sicences, unlike many of his colleagues. His wife Maria died in 1923 in Petrograd at age 24, supposedly of cancer or radiation poisoning. Her ex-husband, Alexander Liverovsky, a Tsarist railroad engineer, was arrested repeatedly but released because of technical skills and his family's links with Lenin and Dzerzhinsky. He was released from the Peter & Paul Fortress (1995 stamp) without falling into one of the mass graves.

2001 Soviet actors including Mikhail Zharov (father-in-law arrested in the Doctors' Plot), Fania Ranevskaya (close friend of murdered director Solomon Mikhoels), Nikolai Kryuchkov (acted in various Cheka-related movies), and Lyubov Orlova (whose husband was exiled then later sent to the camps).

2001 Arkady Raikin, actor. His wife Ruth Ioffe's uncle Abram, a physicist, lost his job in Stalin's anti-Jewish "Doctors' Plot" (see the 2018 Ioffe Institute stamp).

2003 A.P. Alexandrov, physicist, deputy director of Beria's atomic bomb program. His wife and co-worker Antonina Mikhailovna Zolotareva died in 1947, maybe due to radiation. The two were from Kyiv. Mikhail Vasilievich Zolotarev in Ukraine, the only name on a 15 September 1937 kill list, may be her father. [21]

172

2003 I.V. Kurchatov, director of Beria's institute, oversaw many imprisoned scientists, worked with the Gulag camp system to mine and process radioactive materials.

2003 Aram Khachaturian, music composer who was censured. Ethnically Armenian, he was born and raised in Tbilisi and was a teenager when the Bolsheviks invaded. Various Khachaturians and Khachatrians in the 1937-38 kill lists for Georgia/Armenia seem related to Aram, perhaps not members of his most immediate family. [21]

2003 Ernst Krenkl, radio operator for polar expeditions and Arctic research stations. Perhaps 1300 polar scientists were shot or sent to labor camps. Krenkl worked from Siberia during WWII. His first Arctic trip in 1924 was on the ship "Yugorski Shar", confiscated from the former Solovetsky monastery. The fates of his parents (father Teodor E. Krenkel was a well-known German language teacher) are unclear. [195]

2004 Valery Chkalov. When this famous pilot died testing a new airplane, the NKVD arrested more designers and engineers. His children later claimed an NKVD/ Beria conspiracy killed their father.

2004 Yuri Khariton, another atomic scientist. His father died in a Gulag camp after two years.

2004 Svyastoslav Rerikh (or Roerich), artist who escaped from the fledgling Soviet Union as a young teenager with his father Nikolai and family when the Bolsheviks and the Cheka took power.

 2004 Vladimir K. Kokkinaki, airplane test-pilot from Novorossisk. Konstantin, his brother, was another famous pilot. We do not know if his Greek-origin family encountered the Cheka. However, his 1939 state-sponsored biography has no real family information, much like various modern-day online biographies. The NKVD's large 1937-38 "Greek operation" killed thousands of Greek immigrants and descendants. At least two Kokkinakis are listed among the repressed. *[193, 194]*

 2005 Mikhail Sholokov, author. Scholars long wondered who wrote his most famous work, And Quiet Flows the Don. His good relationship with Stalin ended the arrest of Sholokov's best friend. He also had a sexual relationship with NKVD chief Nikolai Yezhov's wife Evgenia at the height of the Great Terror. Sholokov survived, the Yezhovs did not.

 2005 Artem Mikoyan, aviation designer from Armenia. His brother Anastas, Stalin's long-time associate, signed numerous death-lists during the Great Terror and traveled with the NKVD in 1937 to liquidate the Armenian Communist Party. This included killing or deporting tens of thousands of Armenians.

 2006 Armenia. In late 1920 the Red Army invaded Armenia, followed by the Cheka in early December to enforce the new government. Chekist terror was so severe that Armenians rebelled in 1921. They were soon suppressed.

 2006 Dmitri Likhachev—linguistics scholar. Spent five years in labor camps on Solovki and the White Sea Canal, later lived through the siege of Leningrad.

2006 Alexander Yakovlev, Soviet aircraft designer. His father worked for the Nobel Brothers oil firm. It took Alexander multiple tries to enter aviation school due to his non-proletarian background. Somehow, Yakovlev built a close relationship with Stalin and remained unscathed in the purges, unlike many of his peers who were shot or imprisoned. He may have denounced other designers for his own survival. There is almost no information on his parents. His 1969 autobiography says only that his father was in the now-nationalized oil office in Moscow "until the last days of his life". His father was mostly likely repressed. There is a Yakovlev, Sergei *Vladimirovich* in Moscow as No. 30 on the 13 December 1937 kill list. There also is a correctly-named Yakovlev, Sergei Vasilievich listed as shot on 25 October 1937 in Moscow's Butovo Shooting Ground, but his death record states he was born in 1913 in Tashkent. Unlike most death records, this one contains no other data (crime, arresting agency, etc.), which hints that the birth date and location may be false. Perhaps one of these records, or both, is Alexander Yakovlev's father. Neither his father nor mother is in Artamonov's Moscow cemetery lists. *[21, 196, 197]*

2007 Vladimir Bekhterev, early psycho-neuroscientist. His second wife and son were shot in 1937 and his daughter-in-law sent to the camps. He had already received a stamp in 1952, 25 years after he died in 1927. There is evidence that he was murdered for diagnosing Stalin as a "paranoiac". *[198]*

2007 Sergei Botkin, nineteenth-century Russian doctor. His son Yevgeny was the court physician for Tsar Nicholas II, and was eventually shot in 1918 with the Tsar and his family in the Yekatarinburg basement by the Cheka.

2007 Arseniy & Andrei Tarkovsky. Arseniy was wounded as a front-line war reporter, then black-listed & discredited. His filmmaker son Andrei, after years of censorship, chose not to return from a foreign trip. He was allowed to enter only later when his father died.

2007 Nikolai Lunin & Magomed Gadzhiev, submarine commanders. Lunin was arrested in 1938, released a year later. In the war he often falsified official reports of ship sinkings. Once he attacked unarmed Norwegian fishing boats, one of which later rescued a drowning crew member abandoned by Lunin. One fishing crew was taken to the Soviet Union, where several died in Gulag camps. Lunin collected numerous medals and ribbons, and continued to be promoted until his retirement. *[200, 201]*

Gadzhiev drowned in May 1942. He was from Dagestan, a Caucasus region seized and devastated by the Bolsheviks. His father Imadutdin was arrested in 1938 and sent to the northern railroad camp IvdelLag. More than a year after his son became a Soviet Hero, he was informed he would be released, but he remained in camp and died in late December 1943, four days after what would have been his son's thirty-sixth birthday. *[199]*

2008 Lev Landau, physicist. His father was arrested twice. Landau himself was tortured by Chekists in 1938-39. Released because of pleas from scientists, he held strongly anti-Soviet opinions for more than two decades but, lacking options, he continued to work as a Soviet physicist. *[202]*

2008 Ilya Frank, physicist. In 1921 the Cheka exiled his uncle Semon from the USSR with no right of return. The family could not visit or communicate for decades. *[203]*

2008 Valentin Glushko, rocket scientist. Brilliant youth, dismissed from Leningrad State University for inability to pay tuition. Arrested 1937 with many of his colleagues, tortured for a year and a half, then sentenced to Gulag labor but made to work in an NKVD special design bureau instead. Not released until 1944. In a later year, Glushko punched in the face the former co-worker who had denounced him and his now-dead friends.

2009 Zinaida Serebriakova, artist. Bolsheviks seized and burned her artist husband Boris's estate. He was arrested in the Red Terror, released in bad shape, and died. Zinaida went to Paris in 1924 to earn money painting. Two children joined her, two could not. She was not allowed to see them for nearly four decades.

2009 Mikhail Mil, helicopter designer. A classmate denounced Mil—his family had furniture that was too nice. Mil worked in a tannery to reduce his social status then returned to school. In 1936 the NKVD repressed his brother-in-law and Mil's wife lost her job. In the mid-1930s Mil may have worked in an NKVD design bureau, probably after arrest. *[204]*

2009 Andrei Gromyko, diplomat and foreign minister, got his first Foreign Affairs job due to numerous sudden vacancies caused by purges. Later he and **KGB** chief Andropov ran the nation during Brezhnev's long decline. Gromyko's best known words are" Better ten years of negotiation than one day of war". Two of his brothers died fighting in World War II.

As with many senior Soviets, we must piece stitch together an overview of his family. Gromyko and his wife Lydia Dmitrievna Grinevich were from Belarus. His last name derives from his birthplace, the village of Starye Gromyki (now part of the Chernobyl Exclusion Zone). His father Andrei Matveevich apparently spent time in Canada, learned English (which explains how son Andrei began his excellent English), and returned before World War I. It seems he died in Minsk in 1933 during the famine. Andrei Gromyko's 1988 memoirs bypass the 1930s. There are multiple repressed Gromykos from Belarus—some are very likely his relatives. For example, a Mikhail Matveevich Gromyko, perhaps an uncle, was killed in Magadan region in 1938; other Gromykos died in Kazakhstan. *[230]*

As for his wife Lydia, there are many repressed Grineviches in Belarus and Ukraine, and in the deportee zones of Kazakhstan and the Tomsk oblast north of Novosibirsk. Dmitri I. Grinevich was a victim in Kazakhstan—this may be Lydia's father. Unsurprisingly, all the Kazakh Grineviches are male with no data, and all the Tomsk ones are female with no data. Tomsk was a camp destination for wives of enemies of the state in the late 1930s. The male and female ages are similar for marriage or parenting—we conclude that several family generations, possibly related to Andrei Gromyko's wife Lidia, were separated and deported, probably in or soon after 1937; the youngest was an infant girl born that year. *[207]*

2010 Evgeny Fedorov, scientist and explorer. His Tsarist father disappeared. Evgeny ran the Arctic Institute and used Gulag weather data. Denounced in 1947, he was sent to 2-3 years of survey work on Mt. Elbrus.

2010 Nikolai Zubov, officer and ocean scientist. Exiled, re-arrested and imprisoned.

2011 Mstislav Keldysh, mathematician for atomic/ space programs. Uncle and cousin shot, parents arrested (unknown fate), brother Mikhail on the 15 May 1937 kill list. [21]

2011 Dmitri Likhachev. A second stamp for this scholar (see 2006) who spent five years in labor camps on Solovki and the White Sea Canal, and lived through the Leningrad siege.

2011 Ovanes Tumanyan, Armenian poet, died 1923. The Cheka killed three of his sons: Amlik (No. 346, 10 August 1937 kill list), Areg (4 July 1937 arrest; No. 70, 10 June 1938 kill list; shot 14 June 1938), and Musegh (died in Siberia). An Arsen Garich Tumanyan (born 1891) was repressed but his relationship is unclear. [21, 208, 209]

2012 Aldar Tsydenzhapov, a nineteen-year-old sailor, died 2010 in an engine-room fire. Born in Aginsky district, Chita region near Mongolia. His father worked for the security service. Aldar wanted to follow his grandfather Z.G. Vanchikov into the navy, not grasping that most Chita men had been forcibly drafted into WWII. Various Vanchikov relatives in the Chita region were shot in 1938. [213]

2012 Alexei II, Orthodox Patriarch. His father fled the Revolution and settled in Estonia. His uncle Alexander stayed and was shot in 1937. Alexei's family was on an arrest list when the Soviets invaded Estonia but hid in a shed. Later, Alexei, like many church officials, had to cooperate to some extent with the **KGB**. *[214, 215]*

2012 Irina Arkhipova, singer. Some of her early teachers were the famous (and formerly rich) musical/ theatrical Gnesin sisters. The Cheka shot their brother Grigory Fabianovich in 1937. *[216]*

2012 Valery Shumakov, transplant surgeon, died 2008. He spent his later years in Moscow's infamous House on the Embankment, a 1930s apartment building for government officials. From the 1930s through the early 1950s, hundreds of tenants received late-night door knocks that would send them to execution or the camps. His wife Natalya was the daugher of Mikhail Nikolayevich Kaliteevskii from Tver. At least two of her uncles, Evgeny and Fedor, were repressed with 10-year sentences in 1931. *[225]*

2012 Anatoly Koni, lawyer/jurist. He worked more than half a century to develop the Russian judicial system. The Bolsheviks eliminated the entire sytem in 1917, and Koni traded books for bread. In 1919 the Cheka arrested him and seized gold and silver awards accumulated in his life. He was released the next day without his awards. He struggled for the next eight years but dedicated himself to new judicial work as much as allowed, and gave lectures for poor pay until his death. *[217]*

<u>2013</u> Alexander Pokryshkin, highly decorated figher pilot. On the first day of the German invasion, he promptly shot down a Soviet bomber—excessive internal secrecy meant that Soviet pilots didn't know the new model even existed, and thought it was German. He routinely clashed with a superior officer, who tried twice to have the NKVD ruin him. Both times he was exonerated.

2013 <u>Konstantin Stanislavski</u>, a formerly rich theatre director/actor whose factories and house were seized. Arrested by Cheka for one day, he stayed in the USSR as an internal exile too famous to arrest, unlike many of his colleagues.

<u>2013</u> Andrei Tupolev, aircraft designer imprisoned then put to work in an NKVD design facility.

2014 Mikhail Kalashnikov, designer of the AK-47 submachine gun. At age 11 in 1930, his "kulak" family was exiled to a village north of Novosibirsk. His father died that December. Mikhail endured years of cold and hunger, and survived.

<u>2015</u> Pyotr Kapitsa, a second stamp (see 1994 and 2019) for the emigrant who returned on a visit and was forced to stay and work on secret research.

2015 Nikolai Tagantsev, statesman and lawyer. The Cheka arrested his son Vladimir in 1919 for trying to bring food into Petrograd, and again in 1921. Vladimir and his wife were shot despite Nikolai's pleas to Lenin (whom he knew from earlier university days) and despite Vladimir's denunciations of others in a no-execution plea arrangement the Cheka offered, then broke. The broken father was denied exit papers for France, and died or was killed two years later. He supposedly was buried in a cemetery which was later bulldozed.

2016 Vasily Klyuchevsky, historian, died 1911. His son Boris worked in a law office. After the Revolution, Boris was reassigned to legal work, car mechanic, and translator. The Cheka arrested him in 1933, kept him in the Lubyanka for five months, and exiled him to Kazakhstan. *[222]*

2016 Aleksei Maresyev, pilot known for re-entering service as a double leg amputee. Born 1916 in Kamyshin (Volga region), which by his second birthday was engulfed in civil war. The Cheka arrived March 1918 and the war went on. By 1919 his father Peter Andeevich was dead of unclear causes and the British were bombing Kamyshin. His mother Ekaterina Nikitichna kept her children alive through war, famine, and repression. Aleksei went east in his late teens as a construction laborer for Komsomolsk-na-Amure before entering the air force. During the city's construction, it is not clear if he was a prisoner or merely working alongside them as a volunteer or conscript.

<u>2016 Russian Historical Society.</u> The Bolsheviks closed and looted the society in 1917 and repressed many members. Its chief was condemned by a Cheka tribunal and shot while standing half-naked on the edge of a mass grave pit in the Peter and Paul Fortress (see 1995 stamp). The society re-opened in 2004, as a creature of the Russian state to mold and teach approved history.

<u>2016 Mikhail Bulgakov.</u> a doctor who became a writer. Many of his relatives fled the country. His sister Varvara's husband Leonid Karum was arrested and released in 1929, re-arrested in 1931 and sent to the camps, exiled to Novosibirsk, then re-arrested but survived it all. As for Mikhail, he endured the Cheka's searches, bans on his work, and scathing reviews. Stalin protected his life out of interest or amusement. When Bulgakov read the draft of his great work *Master and Margarita* to some close friends, they were frightened by its political undertones and urged him to shelve it. He died before it was published.

<u>2016 Dzhemaldin Yandiev</u>, first national poet in Ingushetia. In February 1944, the NKVD deported him, his remaining family, and half a million other Ingush and Chechens, to Kyrgyzstan and Kazakhstan, where he struggled for more than a decade to survive before moving forward. 100.000 to 150.000 of all deportees died in transit or within a year or two. One source has an extremely incomplete list of almost hundred repressed Yandievs, almost all from Ingushetia, Chechnya or North Ossetia, or their deportation destination of Kazakhstan and Chita (southeast Siberia near Mongolia). *[224]*

<u>2016 Alexander Prokhorov</u>, physicist, born 1916 in Australia to a Ukrainian-born father and Russian mother. There is no evidence for the popular claim that they were revolutionaries who fled Tsarist repression. Gadaloff Road, their isolated address in Queensland, is unique—the surname is found nowhere else in the world. Gadalov, though, is found in Russia and Ukraine, and Chechen Gadalovs were repressed in the 1930s. So, the Prokhorovs were with some Gadalovs in Australia and became Prochoroffs. There was a larger family—Australian records show parents Michael and Maria Prochoroff as of 1919, Alexander's birth, a Clara who died in 1921, and a V. Prochoroff. Alexander's parents returned to the Soviet Union in 1923 but would never leave. Records claim Alexander's father Mikhail Ivanovich died in St. Petersburg (oddly, not Petrograd or Leningrad, which makes the claim suspect). His mother Mariya Ivanovna died in Turkistan town, Turkestan district in the South Kazakhstan region, a place no Russian went by choice. His parents died in their late 50s and his own early record is empty—probably all three were deported to Kazakhstan. They must have deeply regretted returning to the Bolsheviks' brave new world.

<u>2017 Egveny Zababakhin</u>, physicist. A brilliant physics student, his dissertation work caught the attention of the security services. They destroyed his research and sent him to work in various closed cities (built by Gulag slave labor) for nuclear bomb development. Zababakhin later studied non-military uses for nuclear bombs (e.g., excavation, mining, and seismology). The continuing legacy of Soviet experiments of such uses is a number of highly contaminated sites.

2017 Sulom-Bek Oskanov, Ingush pilot, died in a 1992 crash. At six months old in 1944 he and all Ingush were deported to Central Asia. We know nothing of how he survived or if his family did. The popular story of his death is that a navigation instrument failed in low visibility conditions. However, his MiG-29 is an extremely capable airplane but has a short service life and frequent problems. Investigators found a simple but embarrassing cause—a broken mechanical control made Oskanov's plane uncontrollable and the plane tumbled from the sky. [225]

2017 Andrei Karlov, Russian ambassador killed by a Turkish assassin in 2016. He was the third Russian ambassador killed in a century, after Yorosky in Switzerland by a Russian émigré in 1923 (likely arranged by the OGPU) and Voykov in Poland by a Russian exile in 1927 (in retaliation, the OGPU arrested numerous people). The lack of detail on Karlov's background suggests a sad family history. His mother was from Armenia, a country brutalized by Bolshevik invasion, repression, and deportations.

2017 Ivan Aivazovsky, painter, died 1900 in Feodosia, Crimea. His second wife Anna Burnazian witnessed everything that came to Crimea—war, confiscations, Red Terror, famine, purges, deportations—and died during WWII of age, starvation, and grief. He had four daughters from his first wife. Maria may have emigrated, Alexandra died in 1908, Elena died in 1918 during the Civil War, and Zhanna died in 1922 (her Tsarist major-general husband disappeared in 1918, probably shot). Presuably Elena's and Zhanna's deaths were related to the Bolsheviks in some way. Ivan's grandson, Zhanna's son K. K. Artseulov, a skilled Soviet pilot, was arrested in 1933, exiled to Arkhangelsk as a boat mechanic, then rebuilt his life as an internally-exiled magazine illustrator. [226]

2017 Alieva, Fazu Gamzatovna, famous Dagestani poet. Born in 1932 in the tiny village of Genichutl in the mountainous Khunzakh district near Chechny and Georgia. Life was hard—in 1926 the district population was over 29,000; by 1939 it had dropped almost 25%. Kunzakh was in the midst of the 1920-21 Dagestan rebellion—Soviet re-conquest took its toll. Scarce information on her family and early life implies an unhappy story. One of her poems begins: "What am I afraid of? I do not know. All the worst has already happened to me."

2017 Maya Plisetskaya, ballerina, raised by relatives when her parents were repressed. Her father Mikhail ran the Arktikugol Trust (2006 stamp) Gulag coal mine in Svalbard 1932-36, was arrested in 1937 and shot January 1938 at Moscow's Kommunarka shooting ground. Her mother Rakhil was arrested March 1938 with an infant son and sentenced to 8 years in Alzhir (camp of wives of traitors) in the Karaganda mine complex in Kazakhstan. As a dancer, Maya endured with low-paying tours and denial to go abroad. [227]

2017 Sergei Alekseev, lawyer and constitutional scholar who helped write the post-Soviet Russian constitution. His father Sergei Nikolaevich, a statistician, was arrested in 1937 and given a "10-year sentence". In the mid-1990s, Alekseev quit a presidential council and a human rights commission when Russian troops expanded fighting in Chechnya.

2018 Yuri Novitsky, lawyer, professor, and church official. In 1922 the Cheka shot him at night on a roadside along with the Petrograd church leader Metropolitan Veniamin and two others, and buried them in an unmarked grave.

2018 Vladimir Zeldin, actor who kept working until his death at age 101. He devoted his life to music, theater, and film. When the Civil War, famine, anti-Jewish pogroms, and the Cheka came to his home region of Tambov, his family fled 350 miles to Tver. His parents died of unspecified reasons. At 18 Zeldin was arrested by the Cheka but released. His maternal uncle Pantelei Popov was shot, and his 27-year-old brother Yuri died in 1935, maybe due to the Cheka. *[212]*

2018 Olympiad Ioffe, lawyer whose wife and daughter found refuge in the United States in the 1970s. As a result, Ioffe was fired from his job and later exiled to the US.

2018 Ioffe Technical Institute. Abram Ioffe, physicist and uncle-in-law to Arkady Raikin (2001 stamp) lost his job in 1950 during Stalin's anti-Jewish purge. In the 1930s and 1940s, he survived denunciation but saw many peers taken by the Cheka.

2018 Grigory Kisunko, missile scientist. The NKVD shot his father.

2018 Alexander Solzhenitsyn. A rather surprising stamp for the long-time camp inmate, famous author of The Gulag Archipelago, and scathing critic of the secret police state.

2019 Daniil Granin, beloved author who often subtly criticized Soviet bureaucracy. His father was sent to the camps.

2019 Boris Rosing, early television scientist. Arrested and exiled to the north, first to a Gulag logging camp, then to a teaching institute. He is buried in Arkhangelsk.

2019 Ilya Repin, painter. Moved several miles over the border to Kuokkala, Finland when Bolsheviks took over. He refused to return. It seems that in 1925 the Cheka tried to poison him and his family. He died in 1930. In 1935, his 28-year-old grandson Diy foolishly went over the border. He was arrested on 28 Feb, tortured for six months, and shot on 6 August. *[210, 211]*

2019 Pyotr Kapitsa, a THIRD stamp (see 1994 and 2015) for the man who returned to visit his parents and was forced to stay and work on secret research.

2019 Vasily Polenov, artist, died 1927. His daughter Maria wed Vladimir Emilievich Moritz. The marriage ended in 1920. In 1924 Maria somehow exited the USSR and made her way to Paris. The OGPU arrested and exiled her ex-husband Moritz in 1930, the same year that ended Maria's second marriage, to Russian exile Alexander Nikolaevich Lapin, whom she had married in 1926. Maria survived by sewing and later became well-known for artistic soft toys. Ex-husband Lapin, possibly Jewish, appears to have spent time in a concentration camp under German occupation, then died in Paris in late July 1944, a month before the Allies arrived.

Miscellaneous

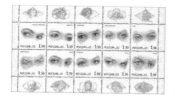

2002 Emotions in eyes, a mostly negative set: excitement, joy, surprise, grief, anger, disgust, shame, contempt, blame, and fear. We include it because of its remarkably oppressive and watchful nature.

2004 Kronstadt tricentennial. In the aftermath of the 1921 Kronstadt Rebellion in this famous naval port, in which Soviet sailors rebelled against Bolshevik rule (including, specifically, the Cheka's reign of terror), many of the surviving rebels and sympathizers went to Solovki, Kholmogory, and other Arkhangelsk area camps.

2005 Russia-DPRK, a joint issue with North Korea, whose own secret police was developed with **KGB** assistance and still runs an extensive camp system.

2008 Aleksei N. Tolstoy, writer, left the Soviet Union in the early 1920s then returned by invitation. First he wrote innovative science fiction, then blunt propaganda about the Revolution and Stalin. He helped write Gorky's notorious book about the White Sea Canal.

2012 Valery Zamaraev, distinguished fireman and rescue officer. Like Tereshkin (2019 stamp) he was born in Sverdlovsk-45 (Lesnoye), a secret city built in the late 1940s by Gulag prisoners to enrich uranium for bombs.

2015 Lena Pillars National Park just south of Yakutsk, a major northern Gulag administrative center. Prisoners going upriver would pass the pillars. The photo on the stamp is across the river near the Tit-Ary camp. Modern boat tours go past the camp cemetery, which is slowly being washed into the river. *[218]*

2015 Alexander Marinesko, submarine captain who sank the *Wilhelm Gustloff* in 1945. More than 9,000 died, mostly thousands of civilians with children fleeing the Red Army. Marinesko got an award and pension but was deeply troubled both before and after the sinking. He was warned repeatedly about heavy drinking, gambling , and prostitution. One writer notes that neither the Soviet Union nor modern Russia explain *why* civilians fled the Red Army: its horrific violence, egged on by Chekist political officers. *[221]*

2016 Barguzin Nature Reserve, whose founders met the Cheka: Entomologist Grigory Kozhenikov went to the Lubyanka in 1933 at age 66 and died of a brain hemorrhage (his student Kuzin later went to the camps). Geographer Veniamin Semenov-Tyan-Shansky lost his classroom in 1932 and his job in 1936 at age 66. His entomologist brother Andrei was denounced for opposing new dams.

2017 Bast shoes, primitive woven bark footwear used in northern forest areas where leather, wool, rubber were unavailable. Gulag inmates sometimes received bast shoes. One group of 200,000 deportees to the frigid north received only 45,000 pairs. *[223]*

2017 The Great Russian Revolution that gave rise to Lenin, the Soviet Union, and a century of Chekists.

<u>2017 Republic of Ingushetia 25 Years</u>. In 1992 Russia created a new republic to support regional stability. Unfortunately, the ensuing Russia-Chechen wars brought waves of refugees. In 2001 President (General) Ruslan Aushev was replaced by a **KGB** general.

<u>2017 Krasin</u>, a Tsarist icebreaker now moored in St. Petersburg. It and others cleared paths to ports like Magadan, where human "cargo" arrived in a special fleet of Gulag ships. *[224]*

<u>2017 Restoration of the Patriarchate</u> celebrates the 1917 election of Orthodox Patriarch Tikhon, a Russian who had obtained American citizenship. The stamp is disingenuous—the Soviets were at war with the church. Tikhon gave autonomy to foreign branches and declared his Soviet loyalty to reduce the damage, but the Chekists continued to seize property, kill priests, use churches as prisons or warehouses, and demolish or blow up cathedrals.

<u>2018 Maxim Gorky</u>, famed writer who later worked with the **OGPU** and **NKVD** on a falsely positive 1929 story about Solovki and a notorious 1934 book glorifying the White Sea Canal.

<u>2018 Russian police</u> tricentennial. The regular police, gendarmerie, or militia were were and are less feared than the secret police, whether the Tsar's Okhrana agents or their Chekist successors.

<u>2018 Karl Marx</u> wrote about causes and solutions for the failures and cruelty he observed in mid-19th century capitalism, industrialization, and urbanization. Lenin created the Cheka to help apply his unique version of Marx's ideas.

Sources
(Some titles and reference information are translated)

1. Abramov, Vadim. 2006. <u>Counterintelligence: Shield and Sword against the Abwehr and CIA</u>. Lubyanka: Open Archives series. Russia: Yauza Publishing. Retrieved from *www.istorya.ru/book/kontrrazvedka/* including "Yan Olsky and Soviet counterintelligence at the turn of the 20s-30s". Retrieved from *www.istorya.ru/book/kontrrazvedka/03.php*

2. Belarus KGB. Biography of Olsky (Kulikovsky), Jan Kalikstovich, Chairman of GPU of BSSR (1921-23). From *www.kgb.by/ru/kratkaya-biografiya-ru/*

3. Borisyonok, Yuri. 2016. "A thief but in state institutions... How a 12-year-old boy robbed Narkomfin and gave Stalin a reason to send his peers to prison." <u>Rodina</u> journal, Moscow: Pravda Publishing. No. 4, pp. 122-125. Retrieved from *istina.msu.ru/publications/article/20225981/* See also *crime-ua.com/taxonomy/term/20287*

4. Demidenko, N.K. entry on p. 65 of <u>Collection of persons awarded the Order of the Red Banner and honorary revolutionary weapons</u>. 1926. Moscow: State Military Publishing House. From *dlib.rsl.ru/viewer/01004483696#?page=65*

5. Construction Chronology of the Moscow-Volga Canal. Retrieved from *moskva-volga.ru/hronika-stroitelstva-kanala-moskva-volga/*

6. Artuzov biography: *deduhova.ru/statesman/artur-hristianovich-artuzov/* Kedrov biography: *deduhova.ru/statesman/mihail-sergeevich-kedrov*

7. Demidenko, Nikolai Ivanovich. Russian online biography at *ru.wikipedia.org/wiki/Демиденко,_Николай_Иванович*

8. Druzhnikov, Yuri. 1997. <u>Informer 001: The Myth of Pavlik Morozov</u>. New Brunswick, NJ: Transaction Publishers.

9. Dzerzhinsky, F. 1921. Note to Special Section on work plan in Caucasus. Doc. no. 371. Retrieved from *www.alexanderyakovlev.org/fond/issues-doc/1018823*

10. Gorky, M. 1935. <u>The White Sea Canal</u>. London: Bodley Head.

11. Jansen, Marc & Petrov, Nikita. 2002. <u>Stalin's Loyal Executioner</u>: Yezhov. Stanford, Calif: Hoover Institution Press.

12. Komarovsky, A. 1939. <u>The Moscow-Volga Canal</u>. Moscow: Foreign Languages Publishing House.

13. Landis, E. 2008. <u>Bandits and Partisans: The Antonov Movement in the Russian Civil War</u>. U. of Pittsburgh Press. Tambov/Syroezhkin/Kedrov, p. 57-8.

14. Maximoff, G.P. 1940. The Guillotine at Work, Vols. I, II. Chicago: Alexander Berkman Fund.

15. Memorial organization. See *www.memo.ru*

16. Pionirskaya Pravda [Pioneer Truth], No. 124, 21 December 1932. Cover page.

17. Puzitsky, S.V. Report by the OGPU operations group on results of work to exile category 2 kulaks, 6 May 1930. TsA FSB RF, f. 2, op. 8, d. 329, ll. 1–28, 31–33, 37– 44. As provided in Viola et al., 2005. Op. cit. Page 289, Document 73. Retrieved from *epdf.tips/the-war-against-the-peasantry-1927-1930-the-tragedy-of-the-soviet-countrysidedac8a214bb4f11b59aa86dec0d798b4890203.html*

18. Rosenberg, Steve. 2002. Stalin's spy stamps stir fears. BBC News, Tuesday April 30. Retrieved 2018 from *news.bbc.co.uk/2/hi/europe/1959071.stm*

19. Sennikov, Boris V. 2004. The Tambov Uprising of 1918-1921 and the De-peasantization of Russia 1929-1933. "Library of Russian Studies" Series. Issue 9. Moscow: Posev. ISBN 5-85824-152-2. See *rusk.ru/vst.php?idar=321701*

20. Sobolevskii, Konstantin. 13 September 1933 letter, p. 3. Retrieved from *topos.memo.ru/en/node/60*

21. Stalin's Kill Lists. Full archives at *stalin.memo.ru/spiski*
    Artuzov, Artur Mikhailovich: AP RF, op. 24, file 410, list 258.
    Artuzova, Inna Mikhailovna: AP RF, op. 24, file 417, list 256.
    Khachatrian/Khachaturian (various) See *stalin.memo.ru/spiski*
    Kedrov, Igor Mikhailovich: AP RF, op. 24, file 377, list 122.
    Kedrov, Mikhail Sergeevich: AP RF, op. 24, file 421, list 13.
    Keldysh, Mikhail Vsevolodovich: AP RF, op. 24, file 409, list 132.
    Olsky-Kulikovsky, Jan Kalitkstovich: AP RF, op. 24, file 412, list 140.
    Puzitsky, Sergei Vasilievich: AP RF, op. 24, file 409, list 197.
    Sokolinsky, David Moiseevich, AP RF, op. 24, file 377, list 127.
    Styrne, Vladimir Andreevich:AP RF, op. 24, file 412, list 134. (crossed out)
    Styrne, Vladimir Andreevich: AP RF, op. 24, file 412, list 186.
    Syroezhkin, Grigori Sergeevich: AP RF, op.24, file 417, list 252.
    Tubala, Iogan Friedrichovich: AP RF, op.24, file 417, list 158.
    Tubala, Elyanora Ignatievna: AP RF, op.24, file 419, list 183.
    Tumanyan, Amlik Ovanesovich: AP RF, op.24, file 410, list 214.
    Tumanyan, Areg Ovanesovich: AP RF, op.24, file 417, list 205.
    Yakovlev, Sergey Vladimirovich. AP RF, op. 24, file 413, list 299.
    Zolotarev, Mikhail Vasilievich: AP RF, op.21, file 411, list 39.

22. For the 2002 counterintelligence commemorative sheet, see: *stamps.ru/catalog/80-letie-obrazovaniya-kontrrazvedyvatelnyh*

23. SVR biographies
  Artuzov: *svr.gov.ru/history/person/ar.htm*
  Artuzov article: *svr.gov.ru/smi/2011/01/nvo20110128.htm*
  Puzitsky: *svr.gov.ru/history/person/puz.htm*
  Syroezhkin: *svr.gov.ru/history/person/syr.htm*

24. Shchelokov, A. A. 2003. <u>Dictionary of Acronyms and Abbreviations of the Army and Special Services</u>. Moscow: AST Publishing, Geleos Publishing.

25. Teplyakov, A. G. 2009. <u>Stalin's Oprichniki</u>. Moscow: Yauza Pub. Ch. 4 Man's Plague: G.S. Syroezhkin. From *memorial.krsk.ru/Articles/2009Teplyakov.htm*

26. Viola, Lynne, Danilov, V.P., Ivnitskii, N.A. and Kozlov, D. 2005. <u>The War Against the Peasantry, 1927-1930: The Tragedy of the Soviet Countryside, Volume 1</u>. Yale University Press.

27. Grigory Syroezhkin boat. Coast guard patrol boats [etc.] Project KS-110. Retrieved from *russianships.info/eng/borderguard/project_ks110.htm*

28. KC-110 boats. Retrieved from *fleetphoto.ru/projects/990/*

29. Antonov, Vladimir Sergeevich. 29 January 2010. <u>And in Spain he was known as Comandante Gregorio</u>. Syroezhkin biographical story. Retrieved 2019 from *nvo.ng.ru/history/2010-01-29/14_gregorio.html*

30. G.S. Syroezhkin. From *www.peoples.ru/state/politics/grigoriy_syroezhkin/*

31. G.S. Syroezhkin. From *ok.ru/group/55014561742875/topic/64521507250203*

32. Syroezhkin Spain photo. Retrieved from *military.wikireading.ru/61169*

33. Regulations: On Work Routines and Duties of NKVD USSR Political Control Employees: Document Selection Group. [Selection & monitoring, procedures & criteria to examine postal documents and packages]. Referenced in Kyiv archives in Dymshits, Mikhail (2016), <u>Soviet Clandestine Mail Surveillance 1917-1991</u>. Regulations retrieved from *www.rossica.org*

34. Brackman, Roman. 2003. <u>The Secret File of Joseph Stalin: A Hidden Life</u>. London: Routledge.

35. Bakatin,V. in <u>Rossiyskaya Gazeta</u>, November 26, 1991, 1st ed., 3, trans. in FBIS-SOV-91–231, December 2, 1991, 21.

36. Colton, Timothy. 2008. <u>Yeltsin: A Life</u>. New York: Basic Books.

37. Belousova, Taisiya. Caches of the great jeweler. <u>Sovershenno Secreto</u> [Top Secret]. 1 Apr 1999. From *sovsekretno.ru/articles/tayniki-velikogo-yuvelira*

38. Artuzov'sKashin memorial photos and location are mapped at: *yandex.ru/maps/10810/kashin/?ll=37.609674%2C57.362405&mode=poi&poi% 5Bpoint%5D=37.608642%2C57.362507&poi%5Buri%5D=ymapsbm1%3A%2F %2Forg%3Foid%3D174534122788&z=18*

For descendants in attendance, see: Monument to the twentieth century legend Artur Artuzov unveiled in Kashin. Tverlife.ru, June 20 1017. Retrieved 2019 from *tverlife.ru/news/v-kashine-otkryli-pamyatnik-legende-khkh-veka-arturu-artuzovu.html*

39. Ardamatsky, V.I. 1982. <u>Selected works in two volumes</u>. Moscow: Fiction Publishing House. See p. 405.

40. Chernyaev, Anatoly. 1985. <u>The Diary of Anatoly S. Chernaev.</u> National Security Archive at George Washington Univ., Washington DC, 2006. From *nsarchive2.gwu.edu/NSAEBB/NSAEBB192/Chernyaev_Diary_translation_198 5.pdf*

41. Gregory Syroezhkin: Camouflage-Man. 2018. 20-min.podcast, Theory of Errors series, RIA Novosti. At *radiosputnik.ria.ru/20180803/1525860065.html*

42. Golysheva, Natalya. 29 October 2017. The smell of a forgotten war: Chanel No. 5 and the "Island of Death" in the White Sea. BBC News Russian Service. Retrieved 2019 from *www.bbc.com/russian/features-41781133*

43. Golysheva, Natalya. 25 December 2017. Red terror in the north: The civil war never ended? BBC News Russian Service. Retrieved 2019 from *www.bbc.com/russian/resources/idt-sh/red_terror_russian*

44. Conquest, Robert. 1971. <u>The Great Terror: Stalin's Purges of the Thirties.</u> London: Penguin. p. 136.

45. Knight, Amy. 1993. <u>Beria: Stalin's First Lieutenant.</u> Princeton University Press.

46. Erofeev, Valerii. Samara history: The great patriotic war: Shooting in the village of Barbysh.   Includes details of Kedrov transport and execution documents from FSB Central archives, cited as documents 617 and 639 in the book <u>State Security Agencies in the USSR in the Great Patriotic War</u>, Vol. 1. (Органы государственной безопасности в СССР в Великой Отечественной войне). 2000, Moscow: Rus Publishing).   Retrieved from *http://историческая-самара.рф/каталог/самарская-история/великая-отечественная-война/расстрел-в-поселке-барбыш.html*

47. Bonifati Mikhailovich Kedrov biography. Retrieved 2019 from *https://ru.wikipedia.org/wiki/*Кедров,_Бонифатий_Михайлович

48. Kedrov, Bonifati. 1986. <u>About the Great Revolutions in Science</u> (О великих переворотах в науке). Moscow: Pedagogy Pub.

49. Bredis, Elena. Another story (Другая история). 13 April 2017. Lipetsk Newspaper. Retrieved 2019 from *www.lpgzt.ru/aticle/61479.htm*

50. The fate of relatives and colleagues of Artuzov. Retrieved 2019 from *www.famhist.ru/famhist/artuzov/00102e0d.htm*

51. Frautchi, Camille Arturovich. Biographical entry. Retrieved 2019 from *dic.academic.ru/dic.nsf/ruwiki/696409*

52. <u>Frautschi</u>. 2008. 49 minutes documentary film about Camill Frautschi (Artuzov). Directed by Oleg Timofeyev and Sabine Gölz. Arbatfilm.com Retrieved 2019 from *vimeo.com/42589057*

53. Gladkov, Teodor Kirillovich. 2008. <u>Artur Artuzov</u>. Moscow: Young Guard Publishing. "Artuzov fell in love", from biographical entry of daughter Nora. in Retrieved 2019 from *www.famhist.ru/famhist/artuzov/00000bc5.htm*

54. Gladkov, Teodor K. & Zaitsev, Nikolai G. 1983. <u>And I Cannot Help But Believe Him...</u> (и я ему не могу не верить…). Moscow: Political Literature Publisher. Retrieved 2019 from *www.e-reading.club/bookreader.php/98216/Gladkov%2C_Zaicev_-_I_ya_emu_ne_mogu_ne_verit'_.html*

55. "Grande Gregory". *www.famhist.ru/famhist/artuzov/000aa29c.htm*

56. Goryachev P.N. 2017 (?) Monograph on Puzitsky. <u>Puzitsky Sergei Vasilvevich: A Look Across Decades</u>. (ПУЗИЦКИЙ СЕРГЕЙ ВАСИЛЬЕВИЧ – ВЗГЛЯД ЧЕРЕЗ ДЕСЯТИЛЕТИЯ) Author is a descendant of Puzitsky and includes quotes from Puzitsky's nephew memoir.

57. A copy of the record of the interrogation of the witness R. F. Melikhova of September 7, 1953. Dated 9 September 1953. From <u>Politburo and the case of Beria. Collection of documents</u> 2012. Moscow: Kuchkovo Field Publishing. Pages 335-339. Original archive: RGASPI. F. 17. Op. 171. D. 467. L. 215-220.

58. Plastinin, Nikandr Fedorovich. Biographical entry. Retrieved 2019 from *www.geni.com/people/*Никандр-Федорович-Пластинин/6000000018023041028

59. Plastinin, Vladimir Nikandrovich. Biographical entry. Retrieved 2019 from *www.geni.com/people/*Владимир-Никандрович-Пластинин/6000000018022953530

60. Plastinina (Nikitina), Alevtina Kozminichna. Biographical entry. Retrieved 2019 from *www.geni.com/people/*Алевтина-Козьминична-Пластинина/6000000018026283052

61. Regarding Artuzov, Inna, and Yezhov, see Gladkov's biography Artur Artuzov. Retrieved from *biography.wikireading.ru/92555*

62. Plastinin, Vladimir Nikandrovich. NKVD biographical entry and NKVD Orders 834, 1310, and unnumbered order of 1 July 1939. Retrieved 2019 from *nkvd.memo.ru/index.php/*Пластинин,_Владимир_Никандрович

63. Plastinin, Nikandr Fedorovich. Biographical entry. Retrieved 2019 from *vk.com/wall-114360762_233*

64, Syroezhkin, G.S. Biographical entry. Retrieved 2019 from *hrono.ru/biograf/bio_s/syroezhkin.html*

65. Savinkov, Lev Borisovich. Biographical entry. Retrieved 2019 from *maitron-en-ligne.univ-paris1.fr/spip.php?article136887&id_mot=3466*

66. Syroezhkin, G.S. Biographical entry. Retrieved 2019 from *rulibs.com/ru_zar/nonf_biography/sbornik/1/j6.html*

67. Ilyukhin, Boris Semenovich. Biographical entry retrieved 2019 from *www.rusperson.com/html/15/RU01006404.shtml*

68. Ilkyukhin, Boris Semenovich professional website. *www.ilyuhin.ru*

69. Musil, Robert. June 1935 Paris speech. International Writers' Congress on the Defense of Culture. "K]einerlei große Kultur auf einem schiefen Verhältnis zur Wahrheit beruhen kann.", from Amann, Klaus. 2007. Robert Musil: Literature und Politik. Reinbek, Germany: Rowohlt Publishers. Page 275.

70. Shavaev, Andrei Gurgenovich & Lekarev, Stanislav Valerievich. 2003. Razvedka i kontrrazvedka: fragmenty mirovogo opyta istorii i teorii (Intelligence and counterintelligence: fragments of world experience in history and theory) Moscow: БДЦ (BDC) Press. Chapter on A. Kh. Artuzov.

71. Russian museum discovers secret order to destroy Gulag data. 8 June 2018/ Associated Press in Moscow. From *theguardian.com/world/2018/jun/08/russian-museum-discovers-secret-order-to-destroy-gulag-data*

72. Puzitsky's confession from interrogation dated 29 April 1937, forwarded by Nikolai Yezhov to Stalin 29 May 1937. Document No. 89, Special message No. 57478. From archives AP RF. F. 3. Op. 24. D. 305. L. 8-23 Retrieved from *apuzit.narod.ru/index/0-7.* Text version also in Goryachev, P.N. *op. cit.*

73. Great Soviet Encyclopedia, 3rd Ed. (1969-78). Retrieved from *bse.sci-lib.com*

74. Montgomery, Isobel. 30 January 2007. Boris Gudz: Russian secret agent who survived purges and party expulsion. Obituary. The Guardian. Retrieved 2019 from *www.theguardian.com/news/2007/jan/30/guardianobituaries.russia*

75. Cook, Andrew. 7 October 2002. To trap a spy. The Guardian. Retrieved from *www.theguardian.com/world/2002/oct/07/russia.artsandhumanities*

76. Komissarov, V.M. Gudz biography and interview. 2017. Lubyanka Historical Readings. (Исторические чтения на лубянке). Society for Study of History of Russian Special Services. p. 82-91. Retrieved from *www.chekist.ru/article/4971*

77. Document No. 56. 25 April 1937. "Special message from N.Yezhov to J.V. Stalin with the proposal to arrest the writer RM. Azarkh". No. 56977. AP RF. F. 3. Op. 24. D. 302. L. 17. From *www.alexanderyakovlev.org/fond/issues-doc/61037*

78. Esipov, Valery and Gavrilova, Anna. 19 October 2012. Interview with Svetlana Ivanova Zlobina, niece-in-law of Boris Gudz. Retrieved 2019 from *www.novayagazeta.ru/articles/2012/10/19/51983-chistyy-pereulok-stanet-esche-i-chestnym*

79. April 28 1937 information. Retrieved 2019 from Moscow-Volga Canal historical site *moskva-volga.ru/hronika-stroitelstva-kanala-moskva-volga*

80. Styrne, V. A. Biographical entry in Petrov, N.V. and Skorkin, K.V. Who Led the NKVD: 1934-1941.

81. Decision of the Council of People's Commissars of the USSR of November 2, 1923 "On the organization of the Solovki forced labor camp". (Постановление СНК СССР от 2 ноября 1923 года "Об организации Соловецкого лагеря принудительных работ"). Moscow. See *www.solovki.ca/camp_20/decree.php*

82. Solzhenitsyn, Alexander I. 1974. The Gulag Archipelago 1918-1956: An Experiement in Literary Investigation III-IV. New York: Harper and Row.

83. On the 100th anniversary of the organs of military counterintelligence "Mail of LPR" released a block of postage stamps. News release from Ministry of Telecom and Mass Communication. Retrieved 2019 from *mslnr.su/789-k-100-letiyu-organov-voennoy-kontrrazvedki-pochta-lnr-vypustila-blok-pochtovyh-marok.html*

84. Giant plastic elephant emerges in Russian city of Arkhangelsk. 9 January 2017. Sputnik News. Retrieved 2019 from *sputniknews.com/society/201701091049398777-giant-plastic-elephant-arkhangelsk/*

85. Sensational loft project "Elephant" in Arkhangelsk closed for unsanitary conditions. 2 May 2017. News29.ru Retrieved 2019 from *www.news29.ru/novosti/obschestvo/Nashumevshij_loft_proekt_Slon_v_Arhang elske_prikryli_za_antisanitariju/63522*

86. Floating hotel-icebreaker "Novorossiysk" will arrive in Arkhangelsk on March 25. 23 March 2017. News29.ru. Retrieved 2019 from *www.news29.ru/novosti/obschestvo/Nashumevshij_loft_proekt_Slon_v_Arhang elske_prikryli_za_antisanitariju/63522*

87. Ahead of the Arctic Forum, an "elephant-record holder" was removed from the embankment of Arkhangelsk. 23 March 2017, News29.ru. Retrieved 2019: *www.news29.ru/novosti/obschestvo/Pered_arktik_forumom_s_Krasnoj_pristani _ubrali_slona_rekordsmena/62329*

88. Nilson, Thomas. 20 January 2019. Russia relocates prestigious Arctic conference away from Arkhangelsk. The Barents Observer. Retrieved 2019 from *thebarentsobserver.com/en/arctic/2019/01/russia-relocates-prestigious-arctic-conference-away-arkhangelsk*

89. In Arkhangelsk, a monument opened to Stalin. 24 December 2016. Echo of the North, Arkhangelsk Regional Public Organization "Ass'n of Young Journalists of the North". *www.echosevera.ru/news/2017/01/16/24928.html*

90. Nilsen, T. 2 October 2017. Stalin bust remains at parking lot in Arkhangelsk. The Barents Observer. Retrieved 2019 from *thebarentsobserver.com/en/life-and-public/2017/10/stalin-placed-parking-lot-arkhangelsk*

91. Kravtsov, Grigory Mihailovich. Examples of typical biographies: *vkr-veteran.com/*Наши_герои/Кравцов_Григорий_Михайлович_11 and from   *ru.wikipedia.org/wiki/*Кравцов,_Григорий_Михайлович

92. Kravtsov original case documents from 1945 can be found on pages 205-207 at *pamyat-naroda.ru/heroes/podvig-chelovek_nagrazhdenie150017162/*

93. Kravtsov Hero: *ru.wikipedia.org/wiki/Кравцов,_Григорий_Михайлович*

94. Russian railway map as of 1916. Retrieved from *upload.wikimedia.org/wikipedia/commons/8/81/Map_of_russian_railroads_191 6.jpg*

95. Zhidkov, Peter Anfimovich. An example of a typical biographical entry can be found at *ru.m.wikipedia.org/wiki/Жидков,_Пётр_Анфимович*

96. Zhidkov, P. A. Army photo and letter to Ekaterina Efimovna Zhidkov, 8 April 1948, announcing Hero of the Soviet Union award. Translated. Army photo and image of original letter from *www.polkmoskva.ru/people/963441/*

97. Zhidkov's original 1943 case documents, images from TsAMO (Central Archives of the Ministry of Defense) are on pages 146-147 at *pamyat-naroda.ru/heroes/podvig-chelovek_nagrazhdenie150011182/*

98. Chebotarev in Hero approval list from June 1945 can be found on page 4 at *pamyat-naroda.ru/heroes/podvig-chelovek_nagrazhdenie46677796/*

99. Chebotarev biographical entry and Hero award images retrieved from *soviet-aces-1936-53.ru/snipers/abc/ch/chebotarev.htm*

100. Abakumov, Viktor Semenovich. Biographical entry from *ru.wikipedia.org/wiki/*Абакумов,_Виктор_Семёнович

101. Krygin, Mikhail Petrovich. Biographical entries.
Basic version: *ru.wikipedia.org/wiki/*Крыгин,_Михаил_Петрович
Glorified version with photos of recent memorials at *samarski-kray.livejournal.com/404868.html*

102. Keller, Bill. 4 February 1989. Major Soviet Paper Says 20 Million Died As Victims of Stalin. <u>The New York Times</u>, p. 1. Based on research and publications of Roy Medvedev. Retrieved from *www.nytimes.com/1989/02/04/world/major-soviet-paper-says-20-million-died-as-victims-of-stalin.html*

103. Goble, Paul. 24 July 2016. Moscow guts Gulag museum while Kyiv gets ready to open one. <u>The Ukrainian Weekly</u>. Retrieved from *www.ukrweekly.com/uwwp/moscow-guts-gulag-museum-while-kyiv-gets-ready-to-open-one/*

104 Plastinina, Rebekka Akibovna. Biographical entry in Russian Jewish Encyclopedia. Online version retrieved 2019 from *www.rujen.ru/index.php/*ПЛАСТИНИНА_Ревекка_Акибовна

105. Shishova, Ulyana Dmitrievna. 2014. Political Propaganda in the Northern Region during the Civil War period of 1918-1920. Murmansk Pedagogical College. Retrieved from *roiarch.com/konkurs/q13.doc*

106. About the newspaper: Our story: Going to the 100th anniversary! <u>Vazhsky Krai</u>. From *old.vk-gazeta.ru/?page_id=117*

107. Artamonov, M. D. 1995. Moscow's Necropolis (Московский Некрополь). Capital Publishing.

108. Kedrov, M.S. 1927. <u>For the Soviet North: personal memories and materials about the first stages of the 1918 civil war</u> (За Советский Север: личные воспоминания и материалы о первых этапах гражданской войны 1918 г.) Leningrad: Priboi.

109. Kedrov. M.S. For the Soviet North. In <u>Stages of a Long Path: Memories of the Civil War</u>. (Этапы большие пути: воспоминания о гражданской войне). 1963. Moscow: Military Publishing, Min. of Defense. Pages 272-293.

110. For description of Gulag experience in Nizhneudinsk and the Taishet region, see *www.taishet.ru/history/sel4.html*

111. Kravtsov, Grigory Mihailovich. Biographical entry. National Security Committee of the Republic of Kazakhstan. Retrieved from *knb.gov.kz/ru/article/grigorii-mihailovic-kravcov-geroi-sovetskogo-souza*

112. Kravtsov, Grigory Mihailovich. Biographical entry and family photo at *ok.ru/group/52600743657541/topic/63460340359237*

113. Dudko, Yuri. 2 August 2019. The last battle of the guard Lieutenant Chebotaryov. In the <u>On Guard</u> newspaper No. 159. Story and file photo at the Belarus MVD website. Retrieved from *mvd.gov.by/ru/news/5793*

114. Lashmankin, V.. The Feat of Mikhail Krygin. Chapter in Kochetkov, Viktor Vasilievich. 1984. <u>Not Quitting the Battle</u>. (Не выходя из боя). Kuibyshev: Kuibyshev Book Publisher. From *document.wikireading.ru/9005*

115. Smirnov, Mikhail A. 1988. <u>About Mikhail Kedrov: Memoirs, Essays, Articles</u> (О Михаиле Кедрове. Воспоминания, очерки, статьи). Moscow: Political Literature Publishers. From *litlife.club/books/284996/read?page=1*

116. ARA feeding plan details. From "Two-week informational summary of the chairman of the Samara Provincial Cheka on the political and economic condition of the province from September 16 to October 1". November 11, 1921. SOGASPI. F 1. Op. 1. D. 516. L. 136,139. Retrieved from историческая-самара.рф/каталог/самарские-тайны-хх-века/1921-год.-документы-1.*html*

117. ARA number of feeding stations in Pugachev county. From "Letter from the chairman of the Pugachevsky executive committee to the chairman of the Samara executive committee V. Antonov-Ovseenko about the situation of the starving population." January 15, 1922. SOGASPI. F. 1. Op. 1. D. 1011. L. 156-157. Retrieved from: историческая-самара.рф/каталог/самарские-тайны-хх-века/1921-год.-документы-2.*html*

118. ARA children's meals. "Information from the gubpomgol about the situation in Samara province as of January 1, 1922." March-April, 1922. TsGASO. F. P-130. Op.1. D. 91. L 67-70. From историческая-самара.рф/каталог/самарские-тайны-хх-века/1921-год.-документы-2.*html*

119. Shafroth information: <u>Hunger. The year 1921</u>. (Голод. 1921 год). From историческая-самара.рф/каталог/самарские-тайны-хх-века/1921-год.*html*

120. Information on William Shafroth: Radosh, Ronald. March/April 2011. The politics of food: How America kept Russia from starving. <u>Humanities</u> magazine. Vol. 43, no. 2. US Nat'l Endowment for the Humanities. Retrieved from *www.neh.gov/humanities/2011/marchapril/feature/the-politics-food*

121. "Blood for Blood", <u>Red Gazette</u>, 1 September 1918.

122. Tubala, Johann Friedrichovich. Biographical entry at *nkvd.memo.ru/index.php/*Тубала,_Иоганн_Фридрихович

123. Tubala, Elyanora Ignatievna. Biographical entry at *ru.openlist.wiki/*Тубала_Элеонора_Игнатьевна_(1902)

129. Kedrov, Mikhail S. 1932. <u>Book Publishing Under Tzarism (The "Zerno" Publishing House)</u>. New York: Workers Library Publishers. Retrieved from *digital.library.pitt.edu/islandora/object/pitt%3A31735066228911/viewer#page/1/mode/2up*

130. Vassiliev, Boris and Kedrov, Mikhail Sergeevich. 1932. <u>Lénine militant illégal</u>. Paris: Bureau d'éditions.

131. Golub, Pavel Akimovich. 2002. "White" terror in the North of Russia. <u>Dialog-Od</u>. Magazine No. 11, pages 71-82. Retrieved from *istoriki.su/istoricheskie-temy/belyy_terror/45-belyy-terror-na-severe-rossii.html*

132. Kedrov, M.S. 1930. <u>Without Bolshevik leadership in the history of the Murmansk interventions: Essays.</u> (Без большевистского руководства из истории interventсий на Мурмане. Очерки) Leningrad: Red Gazette.

133. Plastinin, Vladimir Nikandrovich. 1969. <u>Communist Kedrov</u>. (Коммунист Кедров). Arkhangelsk: North-West Book Publishing House.

134. Stalin, J.V. Concerning the Policy of Eliminating the Kulaks as a Class. From <u>Krasnaya Zvezda</u> [Red Star], No. 18, 21 January 1930. Trans. in 1953. <u>Works</u>, Vol. 12, pages 184-89. Moscow: Foreign Languages Publishing House. From *www.marxists.org/reference/archive/stalin/works/1930/01/21.htm#1b*

135. Demidenko, N. June 22, 1931. "Instructions for members of the OGPU commission to verify the situation of special settlers in the Ural region." From <u>Politburo and peasantry: Expulsion, special settlement. 1930-1940 Book II</u>. Moscow. ROSSPEN 2006 p. 516-522. Archive: TSA FSB of the Russian Federation. F. 2. Op. 9. D. 538. L. 47-56. Typewritten original, signature - autograph. Retrieved from *istmat.info/node/51530*

136. Demidenko, N. June 28, 1931. "'Memorandum' by the head of the OGPU commission N. Demidenko to OGPU assistant head N.G. Nikolaev about 'outrages' in the use of labor of special settlers in the Ural region." From Politburo and peasantry: Expulsion, special settlement. 1930-1940 Book II. Moscow. ROSSPEN 2006 p. 685-688. Archive: TSA FSB of the Russian Federation. F. 2. Op. 9. D. 538. L. 41-46. Typewritten original, signature - autograph. Retrieved from *istmat.info/node/51754*

137. Olsky, J. February 17, 1926. "Memorandum by the head of the Special Department of the OGPU of the USSR, J. K. Olsky, on the implementation by the Air Trust of the production program of 1924/25 and measures to reorganize its work." From Soviet military-industrial production 1918-1926. Collection of documents. "The New Chronograph" Moscow 2005, pp. 537-539. Archive: RGASPI. F. 76. Op. 2. D. 392.L. 67-71. Retrieved from *istmat.info/node/26946*

138. From "A letter from Dobroditsky - an employee of the GPU of Ukraine to the head of the KRO OGPU Y.K. Olsky about returning special settlers." May 31, 1930. From Soviet villages through the eyes of the Cheka-OGPU-NKVD. 1918-1939. Documents and materials. In 4 vols. / Vol. 3. Book 1, p. 384-385. Archive: TSA FSB of the Russian Federation. F. 2. Op. 8. D. 330. L. 24-27. Script. Retrieved from *istmat.info/node/54995*

139. "Letter from employee Dobrodistky of the GPU of the Ukrainian SSR to head of KRO OGPU Ya.K. Olsky about the mass exodus of peasants from exile to places of former residence". May 31, 1930. From Politburo and peasantry: Expulsion, special settlement. 1930-1940 Book II. Moscow. ROSSPEN 2006 p. 469-471. Archive: TSA FSB of the Russian Federation. F. 2. Op. 8. D. 330. L. 24-27. Retrieved from *istmat.info/node/51473*

140. Children as garbage deported by NKVD. Two recountings by F.T. Fomin:

Item No. 1 in:"Statement by the former deputy head of the NKVD of the Leningrad Region F.T. Fomin, to N.M. Shvernik, Chairman of the KPK under the Central Committee of the CPSU." November 29, 1960. From Echo of a shot in Smolny. The story of the investigation into the murder of S.M. Kirov according to documents of the Central Committee of the CPSU. Archive: RGANI. F. 6. Op. 13. D. 71. L. 135-139. Script. Retrieved from *istmat.info/node/60668*

Item No. 9 in: [Appendix 1] "Information compiled by F.T. Fomin for the KPK of the Central Committee of the CPSU". From Echo of a shot in Smolny. The story of the investigation into the murder of S.M. Kirov according to the documents of the Central Committee of the CPSU. 1960. Archive: RGANI. F. 6. Op. 13. D. 21. L. 154-156. Retrieved from *istmat.info/node/60669*

141. "Special report No. 16 of the Secret Operational Directorate of the OGPU 'on kulak operations' on February 15, 1930" (in the ICS, Central Intelligence Center, Lviv Military District, in the Western Region). February 15, 1930. From Soviet villages through the eyes of the Cheka-OGPU-NKVD. 1918-1939. Documents and materials. In 4 vols. / Vol. 3, Book 1. pp. 107-109. Archive: TSA FSB of the Russian Federation. F. 2. Op. 8. D. 41. L. 38-41. Copy. Retrieved from *istmat.info/node/54687*

142. "Telegram from the OGPU leadership to local authorities about the repression of 'kulaks' returning to their former places of residence." June 13, 1930. From Politburo and peasantry: Expulsion, special settlement. 1930-1940 Book II. Moscow. ROSSPEN 2006 p. 479. Archive: TSA FSB of the Russian Federation. F. 2. Op. 8. D. 2. L. 221. Typewritten, signed autographs. Retrieved from *istmat.info/node/51484*

143. Olsky and Yagoda. "Telegram No. 16099 to Minsk - GPU BSSR G.Ya. Rappoport and to Kharkov - GPU Ukrainian SSR V.A. Balitsky." October 7, 1930. From Soviet villages through the eyes of the Cheka-OGPU-NKVD. 1918-1939. Documents and materials. In 4 vols. / Vol. 3, Book 1. p. 493. Archive: TSA FSB of the Russian Federation. F. 2. Op. 8. D. 267. L. 46. Copy. Retrieved from *istmat.info/node/55156*

144. Regarding Olsky seeking information, see "OGPU leadership Order No. 44754 to the local organs of the OGPU on the provision of urgent information on the families of 'single kulaks'." September 21, 1930. From Soviet villages through the eyes of the Cheka-OGPU-NKVD. 1918-1939. Documents and materials. In 4 vols. / Vol. 3, Book 1. p. 463. Archive: TSA FSB of the Russian Federation. F. 2. Op. 8. D. 267. L. 35. Copy. Retrieved from *istmat.info/node/55131*

145. For Puzitsky's written confession, see "Special message from N.I. Yezhov to I.V. Stalin with the attached interrogation transcript of S.V. Puzitsky." May 29, 1937. From Lubyanka. Stalin and the Main Directorate of State Security of the NKVD. Archive of Stalin. Documents of the highest bodies of party and state power. 1937-1938. - Moscow: MFD, 2004, p. 194-200. Archive: AP RF. F. 3. Op. 24. D. 305. L. 8-23 Original. Typescript. Retrieved from *istmat.info/node/31146*

146. Puzitsky's memo on the mass exile. "Report of the head of the operational group of the OGPU S.V. Puzitsky 'On the shortcomings of the eviction of the kulaks' as of May 16, 1930." From Politburo and peasantry: Expulsion, special settlement. 1930-1940 Book II. Moscow. ROSSPEN 2006 pp. 353-355. Archive: TSA FSB of the Russian Federation. F. 2. Op. 8. D. 858. L. 48-51. A typewritten copy of that time. Retrieved from *istmat.info/node/51249*

147. Styrne field report: "Special message of the UNKVD in the Ivanovo region about drunkenness and the decay of some district and rural workers of the Kolchuginsky district, according to data from August 10, 1935 to August 13, 1935." From Soviet villages through the eyes of the Cheka-OGPU-NKVD. 1918-1939. Documents and materials. In 4 vols. Vol. 4, pp. 129-131. Archive: TSA FSB of Russia. F. 3. Op. 2. D. 1021. L. 202-206. Retrieved from *istmat.info/node/57203*

148. Styrne field report: "Special message from G.A. Molchanov of the Ivanovo Industrial Region UNKVD about "shortcomings" during economic and political campaigns in the countryside according to data from November 20, 1936 to November 22, 1936." From The tragedy of Soviet villages. Collectivization and dispossession. Documents and Materials Volume 4, 1934 - 1936. Moscow ROSSPEN Page 890-900. Archive: TSA FSB of the Russian Federation. F. 3. Op. 3. D. 1292. L. 258-273. Retrieved from *istmat.info/node/40954*

149. Styrne field report: "Special message of the Ivanovo region UNKVD about interruptions in bread trade from January 26, 1937 to January 28, 1937." From The tragedy of Soviet villages. Collectivization and dispossession Documents and materials Volume 5 1937 -1939 Book 1. 1937 Moscow ROSSPEN 2004. Pages 124-125. Archive: TSA FSB of the Russian Federation. F. 3. Op. 4. D. 306. L. 206-209. Retrieved from *istmat.info/node/32476*

150. Styrne field report: "Special report of the UNKVD in the Ivanovo-Industrial Region on harvest shortcomings, according to data from August 19, 1935 to August 24, 1935." From Soviet villages through the eyes of the Cheka-OGPU-NKVD. 1918-1939. Documents and materials. In 4 vols. / Vol. 4. pp. 133-140. Archive: TSA FSB of Russia. F. 3. Op. 2. D. 1021. L. 220-229. Certified copy. Retrieved from *istmat.info/node/57206*

151. For Styrne's approval of arrests and executions: "Transcript No. 51 of the meeting of the Politburo of the Central Committee of the All-Union Communist Party of Bolsheviks on approval of troikas and levels of the repressed. July 10, 1937. From The tragedy of the Soviet village. Collectivization and dispossession. Documents and materials Vol. 5 1937-1939, Book 1 1937. Moscow ROSSPEN 2004. Pages 323-324. Archive: APRF. F. 3. Op. 58. D. 212. L. 35-37. Extract from the transcript. RGASPI. F. 17. Op. 162. D. 21. L. 96–97. Script. Subscription copy. From *istmat.info/node/33726*

152. See 151 above for Politburo approvals of repressions.

153. Bonifati Kedrov's letter seeking rehabilitation of his father Mikhail Kedrov. "Letter from B. M. Kedrov to G. M. Malenkov of December 21, 1953." Politburo and the Beria case. Collection of documents - Moscow.: 2012, p. 558-562. Archive: RGASPI. F. 17. Op. 171. D. 473. L. 249-254. Retrieved from *istmat.info/node/22303*

154. Report on the arrival of exile trains. "Special report of the Plenipotentiary Representative of the OGPU in the Northern Territory on the reception and accommodation of exiled and kulak families arriving in trains No. 401, 501, 302, 103, 104." March 5, 1930. From <u>The tragedy of Soviet villages. Collectivization and dispossession. Documents and Materials Volume 2. November 1929 - December 1930</u>. Moscow ROSSPEN 2000. Pages. 282-286. Archive: TSA FSB of the Russian Federation. F. 2. Op. 8. D. 206. L. 143-149. Certified copy. Retrieved from *istmat.info/node/31019*

155. Stalin, J.V. quote about history recalled in Dimitrov's 7 April 1934 diary entry. Banac, Ivo (editor). 2003. <u>The Diary of Georgi Dimitrov 1933-1949</u>. New Haven, CT.

156. The commission report noting Plastinina's mental state is noted in the text and footnote No. 25 of an article by Sokolov, D.V. 8 September 2009. "Mikhail Kedrov and Rebekka Plastinina." State Archive of Socio-Political Movements and Units (the former party archive of the Arkhangelsk Region), f. 1, op. 1, d. 57, l. 57. Retrieved from *d-v-sokolov.livejournal.com/9061.html*

157. Article on Kedrov's interrogation, trial, and verdict: Yakovlev, Georgi. "Pages of history: The 'case' of father and son." <u>Pravda</u> newspaper, No. 48 (25766), February 17, 1989. retrieved from *www.warmech.ru/smersh/kudrin.html*

158. Beaux, Ernest. "Souvenirs d'un parfumeur." Industrie de la Parfumerie 17 Oct. 1946: 228-231. Referenced in Perfumers on Perfume : Ernest Beaux on Fragrance Masterpieces, translated 2013 by Will Inrig, Osmothèque, the International Perfume Conservatory and Museum. Retrieved from *boisdejasmin.com/2013/12/perfumer-ernest-beaux-on-fragrance-masterpieces.html*

159. Bilokin, Sergei Ivanovich. 2017. <u>Mass terror as a means of government in the USSR 1917-1941</u> (Масовий терор як засіб державного управління в CPCP. Second edition. Kiev: Penman Publishing House.

160. Cederholm, B. 1929. <u>In the Clutches of the Tcheka</u>. London: Allen & Unwin.

161. <u>Kholmogorsk Bone Carving</u>. From *www.cultnord.ru/Holmogorskaja_rezba_po_kosti.html*

162. Complaints about Kedrov, starting on p. 41 of Voronova, Olga. (ed). 2018. <u>Pertominsk: Facets of History</u>. Collection of materials on the history of Pertominsk. For Parish of the Intercession Church of Novodvinsk, Arkhangelsk Region, Pertominsk. Arkhangelsk: V.N. Bulatova Publishing House. Retrieved from *docplayer.ru/80723059-Pertominsk-grani-istorii.html*

163. Peskova, Anastasia Alexandrovna. 2014. Does Arkhangelsk need Kedrov Street? (Нужна ли городу Архангельску улица Кедрова?) High school research project retrieved from *nsportal.ru/sites/default/files/2017/04/09/issledovatelskaya_rabota_pestovoy_a.doc* as linked in *nsportal.ru/ap/library/drugoe/2017/04/09/nuzhna-li-arhangelsku-ulitsa-kedrova*

164. Yaroslavl Uprising of 1918. Retrieved from *yaroslavl1918.ru/*

165. Shabanov, Pavel. "Vologda - 1918. The breakdown in toilets and outhouses." Retrieved from *belorizec.livejournal.com/191951.html*

166. Malsagoff, S.A. 1926. An Island Hell: A Soviet Prison in the Far North. London: A.M. Philpot.

167. Vshivkova, T.S. 2017. Vladimir Yakovlevich Levanidov: A scientist and a man. Biographical essay. Federal Scientific Center of the East Asia Terrestrial Biodiversity, Far East Branch of the Russian Academy of Sciences, Vladivostok.

168. Petrov, Nikita. 2001. A decade of archival reforms in Russia. Index/Dossier on Censorship. From *www.index.org.ru/journal/14/petrov1401.html*

169. Fedor, Julie, 2011. Russia and the Cult of State Security: The Chekist Tradition, from Lenin to Putin. Studies in Series. London: Routledge.

170. Transcript of the interrogation of the witness B.N. Merkulov, July 21, 1953. From Politburo and the case of Beria. Collection of documents 2012. Moscow: Kuchkovo Field Publishing. Pages 126-129.

171. Transcript of the interrogation of B.N. Merkulov, 25 September 1953. From Politburo and the case of Beria. Collection of documents, 2012. Moscow: Kuchkovo Field Publishing. Pages 371-378.

172. Crankshaw, Edward. 1956. Gestapo: Instrument of Tyranny. London: Putnam. Page 68.

173. Larkov, Sergei and Romanenko, Fyodor. 2014. Enemies of the People Inside the Arctic Circle. Discussed in Lagnado, Alice. 16 November 2014. How Stalin rewarded Soviet-era Arctic explorers. Retrieved from *www.themoscowtimes.com/2014/11/16/how-stalin-rewarded-soviet-era-arctic-explorers-a41406*

174. Regarding Nikandr Plastining, see Kondratenko, Alexey. 9 December 2016. Mobilized and called upon by the revolution. Orel-Region online publication. Retrieved from *regionorel.ru/novosti/100_letie_orlovskoy_pravdy/revolyutsiey_mobilizovannyy_i_prizvannyy94/*

175. 5-year badges list at *forum.mozohin.ru/index.php?topic=791.140;wap2*

176. See entry on Rebekka and Yakov's father Maisel Akiba (Akim Moiseevich) at *baza.vgdru.com/1/20200/*

177. Bollinger, Martin. 2003. Stalin's Slave Ships: Kolyma, the Gulag Fleet, and the Role of the West. Westport, CT: Praeger. See p. 156 for *Komsomolsk*.

178. Иди и смотри (Come and See) also a superb 1985 Soviet anti-war war movie.

179. Gorky, Maxim. 1929. "Solovki". Feature article in journal Our Achievements, (Наши достижения), 5 (Sept-Oct) and 6 (Nov-Dec). Retrieved as Chapter V from *web.sinn.ru/~gorky/TEXTS/OCHST/PRIM/SU_pr.htm*

180. Biblical verse engraved in the lobby of the Original Headquarters Building of the United States Central Intelligence Agency.

181. Komsomolsk-na-Amure camp map diagram from NKVD files. From *vk.com/30oct_kms?z=photo-165060118_456239049%2Falbum-165060118_257430831*

182. Solzhenitsyn, Alexander. 1978. A World Split Apart. Commencement address at Harvard University.

183. Jan Olsky biographical entry. Yan Olsky and Soviet counterintelligence at the turn of the 20s-30s . Lubyanka Open Archives. Retrieved from *www.istorya.ru/book/kontrrazvedka/03.php*

184. Plastinins and others can be found at: *lists.memo.ru/index5.htm*

185. Styrne's Kyiv address and Syroezhkin's Leningrad address retrieved from *lists.memo.ru/index18.htm*

186. Regarding Styrne's work in Ivanovo, feelings about the NKVD under Yezhov, the burgeoning purge, and the fates of Styrne and his wife, see Chapter 1 (Ivanovo section) of Shreider, Mikhail Pavlovich. 1995. NKVD from the inside: Notes of a security officer. Moscow: Return Publishers. Digital text retrieved from *www.sakharov-center.ru/asfcd/auth/?t=book&num=940*

187. Alexandra Andreevna Ivanova record from *lists.memo.ru/index9.htm*

188. Styrne (Stirne) photo in Zolotaryov, Vadim. 2017. Preparing the conduct of the Polish operation in the Kharkiv region, August 1937. Online monograph retrieved from *www.historians.in.ua/index.php/en/doslidzhennya/2282-vadim-zolotarov-yak-gotuvalosya-provedennya-polskoji-operatsiji-v-kharkivskij-oblasti-u-serpni-1937-roku*

189. From Janis Zile, "Ballad of souls in torment." Written in Vorkuta, winter 1950/51. Translated in We Sang Through Tears. 1999. Riga, Latvia: Janis Roze Publishers.

190. Correspondence from Maria Gudz to Yezhov about returning Galina from exile. Retrieved from *pkk.memo.ru/letters_pdf/002425.pdf*

191. For recollections about the Gudz family and their building, see Soloviev, Sergei. Chisty Lane (1934–1937)—life between arrests. (Чистый переулок (1934–1937) — жизнь между арестами). Retrieved from *old.topos.memo.ru/chistyy-pereulok-1934-1937-zhizn-mezhdu-arestami*

192. Bromage, Bernard. 1933, revised 1956. Man of Terror: Dzerzhinski. London: Peter Owen Ltd.

193. Brontman L. 1939. Vladimir Kokkinaki. Moscow: Military Publishing House of the NPO of the USSR. Retrieved from *militera.lib.ru/bio/brontman_lk_kokkinaki/index.html*

194. Repressed people identified with Greek surname Kokkinaki. See *bessmertnybarak.ru/search/?query=Коккинак*

195. Romanenko, Fedor A. 2010. Enemies of the People: Beyond the Polar Circle. [«Враги народа» за Полярным кругом (сборник)]. Paulson Publishing.

196. Yakovlev, A.S. 1969. The Purpose of Life (notes of an aircraft designer). Moscow: Publishing House of Political Literature. Retrieved from *biography.wikireading.ru/92051*

197. Yakovlev, Sergei Vasilievich (supposedly born 1913, Tashkent). Butovo death record retrieved from *bessmertnybarak.ru/books/person/442592/*

198. Lerner, V., Margolin, J., and Witztum, E. 2005. Vladimir Bekhterev: his life, his work, and the mystery of his death. History of Psychiatry, Vol. 16, No. 2, pp. 217–227.

199. Record of Magomed Gadzhiev's father: *bessmertnybarak.ru/gadzhiev_imadutdin_magomedovich/*

200. Lunin falsification and decorations: *ru.wikipedia.org/wiki/Лунин,_Николай_Александрович_(контр-адмирал)*

201. Sorokazherdyev, Vladimir. 26 March 2005. Lunin against the Norwegian motorboats. Evening Murmansk newspaper. Retrieved from *b-port.com/mass-media/vm/492/9223*

202. Davidovich repression, see: *bessmertnybarak.ru/Landau_Lev_Davidovich/*

203. Frank, Alexander. Memoir of father Ilya Frank. Retrieved from *berkovich-zametki.com/2009/Zametki/Nomer1/Frank1.php*

204. Borisova, V.A. 2016. Mikhail Leontievich Mil. Moscow: Komsomolska Pravda Publishing.

205. Tzouliadis, T. 2008. The Forsaken: An American Tragedy in Stalin's Russia. New York: Penguin Press.

206. Grinevich, Emil Mikhailovich Repression record retrieved from *bessmertnybarak.ru/books/person/833132/*

207. For various repressed Gromyko individuals from Belarus, see
bessmertnybarak.ru/search/?query=Громыко

For Grinevich men repressed in Kazakhstan, and women in Tomsk oblast (wives of enemies of the state were sent most often sent to camps in Karaganda or Tomsk), see
bessmertnybarak.ru/search/?query=Гриневич&number=5
bessmertnybarak.ru/search/?query=Гриневич&number=6

208. Areg Tumanyan: See *bessmertnybarak.ru/books/person/836389/*
Arsen Garich Tumanyan: See *bessmertnybarak.ru/books/person/1813043/*

209. For Ovanase Tumanyan information, see the Toumanian Museum (Yerevan, Armenia) Museum website: *toumanian.am*
The fates of his children, including repressed sons Areg, Arsen, and Musegh, are retrieved from *toumanian.am/tangaran/biography.php?clear=1&cont=5*

210. Borodina, T.P. 2011. The Finnish Detective police supervision for I. E. Repin and his family (based on the materials of the Finnish National Archives). In Baryshnikov & Krotov (Eds.) St. Petersburg and the Countries of Northern Europe, Proceedings of the Twelfth Annual Conference. St. Petersburg: Russian Christian Academy for Humanities Publishing House. Pages 33-45.

211. For Diy Repin's death record, including the recounting of a possible 1925 attempt to poison his grandfather: *bessmertnybarak.ru/Repin_Diy_Yurevich/*

212. Zeldin recounts arrest as part of a longer interview: Zeldin remembers Jewish pogroms. Originally at : *jewish.ru/culture/press/2010/02/news994282545.php*. Retrieved 2019 from Wayback Machine:
web.archive.org/web/20150627050057/http://www.jewish.ru/culture/press/2010/02/news994282545.php

213. For various Chita-region Vanchikovs shot in 1938 (like Zhigmit, Lombo and Sombo Vanchikov), see *bessmertnybarak.ru/search/?query=*Ванчиков

214. Regarding Alexei II's uncle Alexander and death, see: *geni.com/people/Alexander-Alexandrovich-Rüdiger/6000000020469532288*

215. Interview with Alexei II. Vater, Tarmo. 5 December 2008, The Estonian who led 80 million Orthodox believers. Eesti Ekspress (Estonian Express). Retrieved from *ekspress.delfi.ee/kuum/eestlane-juhtis-80-miljonit-oigeusklikku?id=27683925*

216. Gnesin, Grigory Fabianovich. Execution information retrieved from *bessmertnybarak.ru/Gnesin_Grigoriy_Fabianovich/*

217. Sashonko, V. N. Anatoly Fedorovich Koni in Petersburg-Petrograd-Leningrad Retrieved from *vivovoco.astronet.ru/VV/PAPERS/BIO/KONI/BIOKON_1.HTM*

218. Tit-Ary cemetery near Lena Pillars: See *mapofmemory.org/14-17*

219. Ivanovka census data retrieved from: *ru.m.wikipedia.org/wiki/*Ивановка_(Ивановский_район,_Амурская_область)

220. Mikhail Galushkin: *bessmertnybarak.ru/books/person/531781/*

221. Sokolov, Boris. 10 March 2008. Sunken Myth. Graniru.org. Retrieved from *graniru.org/War/m.134310.html*

222. For info on Boris Klyuchevsky, see 1933 letter from his housekeeper Maria Manukhina seeking guidance: GARF. F. P-8409. Op. 1. D. 982. S. 170. Retrieved from *pkk.memo.ru/letters_pdf/002050.pdf*

223. Regarding bast shoe allotment to "special" settlers, see a 1931 report to the Gulag director, page 109 of Frierson, Cathy and Vilensky, Semyon. 2010. Children of the Gulag. New Haven: Yale University Press.

224. For repressed Yandievs, see *bessmertnybarak.ru/search/?query=*яндиев

225. Regarding the mechanical failure of Oskanov's MiG-29 conclusion of the crash investigation report, see *russian7.ru/post/pochemu-pervym-geroem-rossii-stal-urozh/* which draws on the book "General Oskanov's MiG: Memories and Thoughts" by historian Visin-Girey Khasanovich Tankiev (2010, Magas).

226. Konstantin Konstaninovich Artseulov biography. Retrieved from *volyntimes.com.ua/news/1054*

227. Plisetskaya's parents repression records can be found at
bessmertnybarak.ru/search/?query=Плисецк

228. Regarding Maria, seesee Severyukhin, Dmitry. 2012. Biographical entry for
Polenova, Maria Vasilievna. On website "Art and Architecture of the Russian
Abroad:. Retrieved from *artrz.ru/places/1804660654/1805067824.html*

224. Bollinger, Martin. 2003. <u>Stalin's Slave Ships</u>. Annapolis: Naval Institute Press.

225. Evgeny and Fedor Nikolaevich Kaliteevskii relation traced through *geni.com*.
The repression of these two brothers is identified at
bessmertnybarak.ru/search/?query=Калитеевски

226. Rayfield, D. 2004. <u>Stalin and His Hangmen</u>. New York: Random House.

227. Nikandr Plastinin's record identifying him as a resident of Borzya, an exile or
camp destination, retrieved from *bessmertnybarak.ru/books/person/758773/*

228. Plastinin's new wife in Borzya, Anna Dreisenstock. Retrieved from
*ru.wikipedia.org/wiki/*Дрейзеншток,_Анна_Мироновна

For arrest records for Anna and a relative (a brother with incorrect patronymic
or a husband), see *bessmertnybarak.ru/search/?query*=Дрейзеншток

229. Nikandr Plastinin railway police work and conflict with co-worker in Chita:
See Komissarov, Boris Ilyich. 2017. <u>The Truth of a Terrible Time 1938-1947</u>
(Правда страшного времени). Publisher "Literally" (Bukvalno). Plastinin
excerpts retrieved from *www.litmir.me/br/?b=590919*

230. Repressed Gromyko names: *bessmertnybarak.ru/search/?query*=громыко

231. Details of Bubnov's death:
Shkurkin, Mikhail. 2012. On the 140th birthday of Ivan Grigorievich
Bubnov. Balakhnin Museum of History and Art. Retrieved from
*web.archive.org/web/20150112162023/http://www.balamus.ru/index.php?op
tion=com_content&view=article&id=238:bub140&catid=47:kalend&Itemid=
62*

Details of Bubnov's death and wife's name: Bubnov, I.G. biographical /
cemetery article. Originally *on www.funeral-spb.ru*, retrieved from
*web.archive.org/web/20120322201303/http://funeral-
spb.ru/necropols/smolenskoep/bubnov/*

Details of wife and transfer of grave from Preobrazhensky Jewish Cemetery:
Page 28 of Piryutko, Yuri. <u>Historical Cemeteries of St. Petersburg</u>. Digital
copy retrieved from *iknigi.net/avtor-yuriy-piryutko/47270-istoricheskie-
kladbischa-sankt-peterburga-yuriy-piryutko/read/page-28.html*

232. Regarding Yuri Chaika's corruption, beginning as a prosecutor in Nikolaevsk-na-Amur, see as an example the variety of newspaper articles merged at and retrieved from *debri-dv.com/article/212*

233. For Bochkov testimony in 1954 Beria case about fabricating an "authorization" for killing Kedrov and others, see "Copy of the transcript of interrogation of witness V.M. Bochkov of January 25, 1954." From <u>Politburo and the Beria case. Collection of documents</u> - Moscow .: 2012, p. 567-572. Archive: RGASPI. F. 17. Op. 171. D. 474. L. 39-46. Retrieved from *istmat.info/node/22307*

234. For numerous repressions of Syroezhkin surnames, including from Volkovo or the broader Saratov oblast, see *lists.memo.ru/index18.htm* as well as *bessmertnybarak.ru/search/?query=*Сыроежкин Search also for Syroeshkin and Syroezhkina.

235. The "Chekist" also appears in a heavily retouched 27 April 1937 newspaper montage photo credited to A. Egorova. Egorov took several other pictures that day which entered into official archives. See *ikuv.ru/pervaya-flotiliya-kanala-moskva-volga/*

236. The "Chekist II" appears in a Solovki camp photo album given to Leningrad party leader Sergei Kirov sometime before his murder in December 1934. Retrieved from *oppps.ru/sovetskij-lager-osobogo-naznacheniya.html*

Main Index

	ROLE	FATE	PAGES
OLSKY, JAN	Chekist	shot	23-5, 30, 62, 65-8, 70, 96, 102, 160
Olsky, unknown	wife	camp	68
Olsky, unknown	son	orphanage?	68
Olsky, unknown	son	to relatives?	68
PUZITSKY, SERGEI	Chekist	shot	19, 23-25, 36, 62, 66, 69-73, 87, 89, 96, 98, 102, 108, 160
Puzitsky, Vladimir	brother	arrest, lived	72
Sereda, Larisa	wife	camp, lived	72-3
Sereda, unknown	mother-in law	camp, died	72
STYRNE, VLADIMIR	Chekist	shot	19, 23-5, 66, 75-82
Styrne, Alexandra	wife, Chekist	shot	79, 81-2, 96, 98, 102, 105, 160
Sokolinsky, David	Styrne's Chekist Kyiv predecessor	shot	78, 81
SYROEZHKIN, GRIGORI	Chekist	shot	19, 23-25, 36, 44, 70, 83-91, 96-98, 102, 106, 160

2018 STAMP MEN

	ROLE	FATE	PAGES
ABAKUMOV, VIKTOR	SMERSH chief	shot	126, 129, 144-6, 153, 160
CHEBOTAREV, VASILY	SMERSH agent	died in war	126-29, 140-43, 149, 151, 155, 160

OTHERS IN MAIN TEXT

	ROLE	FATE	PAGES
Andropov, Yuri	USSR leader, Chekist	died in office	98, 103, 106
Bakatin, Vadim	last KGB boss of USSR	retired	103
Beaux (Bo), Ernest	created Chanel No. 5 perfume	went to France	31-2, 48
Beria, Lavrenty	secret police chief, Chekist	shot	11, 39-40, 44-5, 61, 102, 105, 120, 121, 122, 127, 145
Brezhnev, Leonid	USSR leader, Chekist in youth	died in office	103, 105-6, 107
Chernenko, Konst.	USSR leader, Chekist in youth	died in office	106
Dzerzhinsky, Felix	Cheka founder	likely poisoned	2, 9, 19, 25, 28, 61, 62, 70, 87, 93, 96, 98, 101, 111, 113, 122
Gorbachev, Mikhail	USSR last leader	retired	103, 107, 163
Kalinin, Mikhail	chair of Central Committee	died of cancer	111
Kalinina, Ekat.	wife	camp, lived	111
Khruschchev, Nikita	USSR leader, Cheka colleague	left office	25, 45, 105, 107
Kryuchkov, Vladimir	KGB chief	lived	103
Lenin, Vladimir	USSR founder	maybe poisoned	2, 4, 6-11, 28, 32, 38, 42-5, 48, 76, 103, 123
Krupskaya, N.	Lenin's wife	maybe poisoned	6-7
Makarova, Tamara	actress	Lived	160-2
Gerasimov, Sergei	husband	lived	160-1
Makarova, Lyud.	sister	shot, exile or camp	161
Tsvilko, Adolf	Lyudmila's hus.	shot, exile or camp	161

Appendix Index

NAME	STAMP	FATE	PAGES
Ilyushenko, Alexei	2017	prosecutor	165-6
Ingushetia	2017	repressed region	169,183 184,191
Ioffe, Olympiad	2018	exiled	187
Ioffe Technical Institute	2018	namesake repressed	187
ITAR-TASS	2004	cover agecy for Chekists	164
Journalism	2003	repressed	164
Kabardino-Balkara		repressed region	169
Kalashnikov, Mikhail	2014	family exiled	181
Kapitsa, Pyotr	1993 2015 2019	slave scientist	171 181 188
Karlov, Andrei	2017	assassinated	188
Kazannik, Aleksei	2017	prosecutor	1656
Keldysh, Mstislav	2011	family repressed	179
Khachaturian, Aram	2003	censured	173
Khariton, Yuri	2004	father to camp	173
Kisunko, Grigory	2018	father shot	187
Kitanin, Roman	2019	Chekist	170
Klyuchesvky, Vasily	2016	son exiled	182
Koen (Cohen), Leontina	1998	Chekist	167
Koen (Cohen), Morris	1998	Chekist	167
Kokkinaki, Vladimir	2004	test-pilot, like his brother Konstantin. The Cheka repressed many of their fellow ethnic Greek	174
Komsomol	2018	used for Cheka recruiting	166
Koni, Anatoly	2012	repressed	180
Krasikov, Alexander	2018	Chekist	169
Krasikov, Peter	2017	Chekist, procurator	165

NAME	STAMP	FATE	PAGES
Moscow Metro	2005	slave-built	161
NKVD special camp no. 7 (former Sachsenhausen)		camp	168
Norilsk Nickel	2015	slave-built	162
North Korea	2005	advised by Chekists	189
Novitsky, Yuri	2018	shot	186
Novosibirsk	2003	Gulag city	164
Ordzhonikidze, Sergo Command School	2018	namesake shot	166
Orlova, Lyubov	2001	spouse: camp	172
Oskanov, Sulom-Bek	2017	family repressed	185
Pankratiev, Ivan	2017	Chekist procurator	165
Peter & Paul Fortress	1995	mass graves	160, 172, 182
Plekhanov Georgi Acad. of Economics	2007	namesake possibly shot	161
Plisetskaya, Maya	2017		186
Pokryshkin, Alexander	2013	repression attempted	181
Polenov, Vasily	2019	daughter fled, former son-in-law exiled	188
Population Census	2002	reminds of Stalin's census	160
Procurator General	2017	Chekist prosecutors	165-66
Prokhorov, Alexander	2016	family likely exiled	184
Putin, Vladimir	2000 2012 2018	Chekist	167 167 169
Putintsev, A. M.		sent to camp	171
Raikin, Arkady	2001		172
Ranevskaya, Fania	2001	friend of Cheka victim	172
Raskova, Marina	2012	Chekist	167
Rekunkov, Alexander	2017	prosecutor	165

Made in the USA
Columbia, SC
27 January 2020